CHICAGO'S ITALIANS
IMMIGRANTS, ETHNICS, AMERICANS

In memory of

Ella F. Carraro

These 105 people are the descendants of Firmino and Gelinda Dalpiaz, who emigrated to Melrose Park from Trento, Italy, in 1920 and 1924 respectively. They were married in 1924 in the Church of Our Lady of Mount Carmel. They had ten children, including two Scalabrinian priests who trained at the Sacred Heart Seminary, Father Gino and Father Alex. Firmino died in 1970, Gelinda in 1999 at the age of 97. Father Gino is director of the Italian Cultural Center and Father Alex serves South-American immigrants in Orlando, Florida.

COVER: *The Augusta Corratini–Charles Rufo wedding in Chicago Heights in 1929 included 27 people in the wedding party. From left to right are the following: (first row) Yolanda Giannetti Candeloro, two unidentified people, Charles Rufo, Augusta Corratini, Miss Geraci, Nick Macaluso; (second row) Lucy D'Angoia, Agusta Apponi Passarelli, Susie Lolli, Lucy Rufo, Virginia Aprati, Angelina Cipolla, Giselda Canali; (third row) Tip Capolongo, Frank Capua, Tony Rufo, Pete Corratini, Romolo Cipolla, Louis Canali, Angelo Tiberi. The miniature groom and bride were Joe Panici and Mary Giannetti Santori. Tradition has it that there were well over 1,000 guests at the reception held at the Masonic Lodge over a three day period. Reportedly, as a result of the bash, the Masonic Temple stopped renting out its facilities for weddings.*

THE MAKING OF AMERICA

Chicago's Italians

Immigrants, Ethnics, Americans

Dominic Candeloro

ISBN 978-0-7385-2456-6

Published by Arcadia Publishing,
Charleston SC, Chicago IL, Portsmouth NH, San Francisco CA

Printed in the United States

Library of Congress control number: 2003111661

For all general information contact Arcadia Publishing at:
Telephone 843-853-2070
Fax 843-853-0044
E-Mail sales@arcadiapublishing.com
For customer service and orders:
Toll-Free 1-888-313-2665

Visit us on the Internet at www.arcadiapublishing.com

CONTENTS

ACKNOWLEDGMENTS

This book in many ways is the accumulation of thousands of personal experiences, growing up Italian in the Chicago area. Since 1977, I have had the privilege of studying Italian-American culture as a profession. I have met so many people along the way in meetings, interviews, at dinners, and at festivals. Most of them opened up their lives to me and transferred to me whatever wisdom there might be in this book.

The pioneering work of Rudolph Vecoli and the Chicago collections he maintains at the Immigration History Research Center have been very useful to me, especially when dealing with the early years and World War II. The World War II research ideas shared with me by Gary Mormino and the late George Pozzetta were also valuable.

The works of Giovanni Schiavo and Humbert Nelli are loaded with information that I used in writing this book. I owe them a debt of gratitude. Father Gino Dalpiaz and the staff at the Italian Cultural Center, Daryl Marchioretto, and Christina Harrison were very gracious in extending to me countless favors as I gathered up material from which to write this book.

My good friends, the Two Tonys, Tony Scariano and Tony Sorrentino, answered my questions and sat for interviews. Sorrentino's two books on the Chicago Area Project and the Joint Civic Committee guided a lot of my writing. Rose Ann Ciambrone and her father, my former boss, ex-Mayor Angelo Ciambrone, also gave me useful input.

Leonora LiPuma of the Chicago Italian American Chamber of Commerce was very accommodating in giving me access to the photos and the bound volumes of the Chamber's *Bulletin*. Joe Glimco, Bob Rubinelli, Daniel Niemiec, Paul Giuliano, and the Italian-American collection at the University of Illinois at Chicago Daley Library also provided photos.

Paul Basile again gave me access to the photo archives of the *Fra Noi* and I also thank him for putting together the *1995 Italian American Directory*, which I used repeatedly.

My good wife, Carol Cutlip Candeloro, dutifully read and re-read every draft. I can never repay her for that sacrifice.

Thanks to all. Dominic Candeloro

INTRODUCTION

Italians have been in Chicago since 1850. Italians were present during the Civil War and the Great Chicago Fire. They played a role in the massive industrial expansion of the city as the railroad capital of the United States. As unskilled and often illiterate workers they started at the bottom, enduring more than their share of racial and ethnic stereotyping and discrimination. They lived in over-crowded housing and worked long hours under poor conditions for small wages. They also tended their gardens, did for themselves, and arranged to bring their relatives to join them in Chicago. And some Italians found rapid success in importing fruit and vegetables.

Immigrant Italian colonies were the object of the humanitarian efforts of Jane Addams at Hull House. At the same time, Italians built and developed a score of neighborhoods in a pattern that defined the Chicago landscape—Italian Catholic churches, parochial schools, ethnic-oriented groceries, butchershops, barbershops, clubs, and newspapers. Italian and other bootleggers in Chicago captured the imagination of the American public during the 1920s prohibition era. In the 1930s, Chicago Italians basked in the glory of Italo Balbo's transoceanic flight to Chicago and the popular acceptance of Mussolini's fascism. During the World War II period, Italian Americans were among those descended from enemy aliens and among the groups who answered the United States military draft in massive numbers. It was an Italian émigré, Enrico Fermi, who did the basic research in Chicago that resulted in the atomic bomb, the weapon that hastened the conclusion of World War II.

The lives of Italian Americans were changed dramatically by urban development that took place after World War II. The building of expressways disrupted Little Italies, while the housing boom and suburbanization lured the second generation out of the Italian enclaves in which they had grown up. As Chicago Italian families move into the fourth and fifth generations and intermarry with other ethnics to become part of the managerial and professional middleclass, the challenges to ethnic retention have been strong. On the other hand, the wartime devastation of Italy sparked a renewed migration of ambitious young people who reignited the embers of Italianitá.

Since the 1960s, cultural diversity and pluralism have become fashionable and Chicago Italian-American organizations like the Joint Civic Committee of Italian

Americans have benefited. Their efforts to end defamation, demand respect, and to disseminate Italian culture have won them a niche in Chicago's ethno-political arena. The Italian government has also promoted Italian language and culture to Italian Americans and the general American market to enhance tourism, commerce, and the general political image of Italy. The projects of Italian Americans, such as the *Fra Noi* newspaper, Villa Scalabrini, the Italian Cultural Center, Casa Italia, and Italidea continue to draw strength from these trends. Influential Italian-American business leaders and politicians in the population of 500,000 Italian Americans in Cook County have also come to the aid of the cause.

For 150 years in Chicago, Italians have been there every step of the way, an integral, if not dominant, part of the story. As time passes and memories fade, the need to recapture the past increases. My *Images of America: Italians in Chicago* and my *Voices of America: Italians in Chicago*, and now this book attempt to portray the social history of Chicago's Italians and to document the exploits of the prominenti and achievers.

This book is offered as a tool to help Italians define themselves and to understand how the experiences of their ancestors helped to create the world in which they now live. Others will see it as another perspective on Chicago's history and on American history, or another chapter in world immigration history.

Every published history is a work in progress. Different writers using the same facts would come up with a different emphasis, different interpretations, and different errors. Additions and corrections to this narrative are welcome and will be placed on file at the Italian Cultural Center in Stone Park, Illinois. Send them to me at D-Candeloro@govst.edu. I will place the research materials that I used in writing this book on file in the Italian Cultural Center Library.

As I have worked on Italian American history, I have often wondered what my parents and grandparents would have thought of my efforts. I am even more concerned about what my children and grandchildren will think of my work. This book is dedicated to my ancestors and my descendants.

Chicago Heights

Chapter One

THE BEGINNINGS

Of all the challenges faced by the immigrant to a new land, perhaps the most puzzling is the language gap. Native Americans referred to Chicago as the "Stinking Onion." Even the most unsophisticated Italian immigrants to Chicago must have been amused by the name of the town. Many were even reluctant to utter the name of the city in mixed company. In Italian, *Ci Cago* (pronounced Chee-ca-go) means "I defecate." The standard Italian-American joke was to respond to *Ci Cago* with *E Ci Piscio* (and I urinate). So much for the image of Chicago as a land where the streets were supposed to be paved with gold.

As a rail center, an industrial center, and America's fastest-growing major city, Chicago offered opportunities for immigrants from all nations in the period between the Civil War and World War I. In the mid-nineteenth century it was the Mecca for German and Irish migration; in the early twentieth century, Italians, Russian Jews, and, most importantly, Poles found a place in Chicago. Later, African Americans from the South, Mexicans and Asians, and a steady stream of others added their presence to the city, making it today the home of sizable colonies of over 80 different nationalities. Chicago's black population is second only to that of New York City; at one time or another it has been the largest Lithuanian city, the second largest Polish city, the second largest Bohemian and Ukrainian city, and the third largest Swedish, Irish, Polish, and Jewish city in the world. But it has never been claimed that Chicago had enough Italians to be one of the largest Italian cities in the world.

As in most older American cities, Italian ethnic identity has persisted well beyond the "melting pot," and a sophisticated understanding of the economic, political, social, and cultural dynamics of the city is impossible without careful consideration of ethnic factors. Being part of the complex interaction and outnumbered by the Irish, Poles, blacks, and Hispanics, Italian aspirations for power and prestige have often been thwarted. Efforts at developing internal unity and at building coalitions with other ethnic groups have not offset their numerical weakness. And while Italians have played a significant role, they have never been as important in Chicago's mix of ethnics as they have been in New York, for instance. On the other hand, Italians have claimed their rightful place in the city's public rituals honoring cultural pluralism.

Italians have been in Chicago since 1850, when the census listed four of them. Two Genoese bothers, Frank and August Lagorio, arrived in Chicago and set up an importing business. They were on their way to California, but decided that Chicago's location (where the river meets the lake) on principal transportation routes suited them better. In the second generation, Antonio Lagorio became the first Italian-American physician in Chicago and for several generations the Lagorios played a major role in the wholesale produce business in the city.

Since the distribution of produce is very compatible with the grocery and restaurant businesses, newly-arrived *paesani* often expanded into those enterprises. A neighborhood of Italian families grew up in those early years in the vicinity of Kinzie, Illinois, and Orleans Streets, north of the river. The group consisted of Genoese fruit sellers, restaurateurs, and merchants with a sprinkling of Lucchese plasterworkers. These were joined in the 1870s by a group of itinerant musicians, organ grinders engaged in what some writers referred to as "monkey business." Except for the last group, early Chicago Italians were generally well accepted and economically successful, establishing themselves in the central city and the Near North Side.

The federal census reported 552 Italian-born residents in 1870. According to Judge Francis Borelli, the 1870s migration brought to Chicago Louis Impelletieri, Dr. Joseph Ronga, Emilio De Stefano, Antonio Sbarbaro, and Borelli's father, Antonio Borrelli. The offspring of these early immigrants moved into the professions by the 1920s. They settled around Polk and Canal Streets, but moved west to what became the Taylor Street neighborhood after the Chicago Fire.

In 1890, the census reported 5,685 and in 1900 the number grew to some 16,000 Italian-born residents living in Chicago, which was probably an undercount. Overcrowded living conditions, frequent changes of addresses, and the language problem made Italians and other immigrants difficult to count. As the great migration intensified, the newcomers began coming from the central and southern parts of Italy and Sicily. They were the poor and illiterate country folk displaced by global economic changes and the economic policies of an uncaring government. This wave of almost 5 million unskilled southern immigrants came to the United States between 1880 and 1914. In the early years, most of them were young men, birds of passage, who intended to work for a season or two and return to their families. Many did just that. Others became part of intricate chains of migration that re-established villages and towns in Chicago's neighborhoods and suburbs.

Deprived of decent opportunities to earn a living in Italy, immigrants came to Chicago for *pane e lavoro* (bread and work) and evinced an enormous work ethic. The city was frantically building its infrastructure of waterways, sewage and road systems, the rail network, and housing, trying to keep up with population growth. According to Rudolph Vecoli's thesis, at the turn of the century fully 50 percent of the "gang laborers" on public works projects were Italian. These jobs were grueling, dangerous, unpleasant and dirty, but they enabled many to reconstitute their families in Chicago. The occupations pursued by the immigrants fell into several categories. Railroad laborers and construction workers were in great demand. Jobs were plentiful for hod carriers, mosaic tile layers, plaster workers, stone cutters, and other skilled and unskilled workers (*braccianti*) in the building trades. Lucchesi plaster workers were there in 1892 to construct and decorate the buildings of the Columbian Exposition. And it was Italians who laid the mosaic for the Chicago Public Library in 1890. One oral history source remembered his father and the sewer work he did:

> As a boy, sometimes we'd go downtown. He could spot places downtown along LaSalle Street and various streets downtown where they had dug for underground wiring, I guess or plumbing or that kind of thing. He was familiar with the under part of Chicago, you know, rather than the upper part.

Long hours of drudgery often yielded little pay. Especially for the unskilled workers, conditions were dangerous and job tenure insecure. As poet Joseph Tusiani put it, "This country needs YOU. But this you must not know." Gradually, Italians were able to exert some control over their work in construction. Italians, like the Pontarellis, organized their own firms and won major contracts for sewer and curb construction. On the other side of the coin, Italians like Joseph D'Andrea and later Peter Fosco came to dominate the Laborers' (Hod-Carriers') Union.

In the period before 1900, many Italian immigrants found work through the *padrone* system. Among the more entrepreneurial early immigrants there developed a class of labor agents who often served as saloonkeepers providing meals and beds for workers. Many of them were dishonest and took advantage of the "greenhorns"—taking commissions from both the employer and the employee and extending credit to unemployed workers at unfair rates or selling political jobs. *L'Italia* in 1896 praised Mayor Swift for curbing this kind of bossism that had existed among municipal workers in the sanitation department. Editor Oscar

Durante compared the padroni to slaveholders, only this time the slaves were white and Italian. In a sense, the *padrone* system was a necessary evil in the early days. Gradually the number of *paesani* (fellow townsmen) and *parenti* (relatives and priests) increased, indigenous family/community institutions took over, and the padrone system became almost obsolete by 1900. Vecoli suggests that Luigi Spizziri as early as the 1870s was acting as a good padrone—lending money to hundreds of his Calabrian *paesani* to make the crossing to Chicago.

Nineteen percent of southern Italian women and 13 percent of northern Italian women worked outside the home, a surprisingly high number compared to the much lower rate reported by Yans-McLaughlin in her study of Italian women in Buffalo. It was common for families to take on boarders and this meant that the woman of the house doubled her work at home cooking over a coal fire and doing laundry with a hand wringer. All this was in addition to traditional tasks women did for their families. Italians did for themselves: they maintained enormous gardens, they canned tomatoes for sauce, made wine, beer, and root beer, baked bread, made macaroni from scratch, picked cicoria in the open fields for both salad and boiled greens, made sausage from the meat of freshly slaughtered pigs, kept chickens, kept goats and made cheese from goat's milk, picked mushrooms, prepared delicacies from burdock stalks, made soap from leftover animal fat, and even prepared natural cures for broken bones and supernatural cures for severe headaches (*il mal occhio*). Only about 10 percent of all Italian women in the sample were reported to be English speaking.

Conditions were deplorable. In a disturbing 1892 account by Italian theatrical director Giuseppe Giacosa, who encountered elderly female rag pickers near the grain elevators along the river, he recounted their encounter as he pointed to the trash heap:

> They come every day, rain or shine, to pick out from the filth the value of a few cents: a pair of old shoes, a blouse torn to shreds, waste paper, strips of leather, nails, bullets, wires or iron, and an old bottle of died up medicine. They manage to find a use for everything including wearing the clothes. . . . They also feed themselves from the refuse, finding celery, carrots, cabbage, potatoes half-baked. . . . When asked why they didn't go home and knit for a living, they responded surprised, "And this, who would come and take these things?"

Giacosa ended by praising the Italian bent for frugality. He had come to understand the rag pickers.

A *Tribune* article (1885) speculated that a Neapolitan family could earn $7 from junk iron and rags collected on a summer morning east of Clark Street. While the article showed some appreciation for the recycling service, the stench of the washed out rags hanging on clothes lines was feared as a health threat. The rag picking continued throughout the first half of the century. Anthony Sorrentino vividly remembers the haunting call of "RAG-SO-LINE!" (rags and old iron) from his youth on the Near West Side.

In the early years, many Italian women and girls also worked at home, sewing mountains of coats or pants in dim light for pennies an hour. This was referred to as the "putting out system" and hapless immigrants were often cheated by fast-talking agents. By 1900, large clothing factories replaced the homework and sweatshops. Both men and women were engaged in the needle trades at such establishments as Hart, Schaffner, and Marx. This brought together on the Near West Side a critical mass of perhaps 40,000 clothing workers, a good number of them of Italian background.

Since their take-home earnings in season for a 56- to 72-hour (6 day) week averaged around $3, it's not surprising that workers began organizing the Garment Workers and the Amalgamated Clothing Workers with a strike in 1910. Italian socialists such as A.D. Marimpietro and Emilio Grandinetti were among the leaders in several dramatic Chicago strikes by the Amalgamated Clothing Workers Union. Women also played a big role in this era. Clara Mansilotti, a Kupenheimer employee, emerged in the 1910 strike as a fiery speaker in both languages and a crafty organizer. Other women who led the 1913 United Garment Workers Union strike as shop chairwomen were Joanne Latawic, Giulia Paoli, and Ida Bertacchi. Italians also formed several all-Italian locals of the Amalgamated in the pre–World War I period.

According to Rudolph Vecoli, however, during that prewar era it was unusual to find Italian employees indoors, in factories. A considerable number of Italians did, however, work at the Pullman plant, adjacent to the Roseland Italian colony, and at the McCormick Reaper Plant on the southwest side near the 24th and Oakley neighborhood. Only a minuscule number worked in Chicago's mammoth meatpacking plants, reportedly because they found the work distasteful and they were wary of competing at low wages with African Americans. With the exception of Chicago Heights where Inland Steel, Calumet Steel, and Amsco employed Italians by the hundreds, Italians were underrepresented in the workforce of the great steel mills of South Chicago in the period before 1920.

Though they preferred outdoor work, few seriously pursued agriculture in the Chicago area, despite efforts by reformers to return the former *contadini* to the land. Generations of Italian American women from Chicago Heights served as day laborers, transported in trucks to the South Holland onion fields, where they planted, weeded, and picked the crop. Almost every issue of *L'Italia* carried advertisements for fertile land with abundant water and rail access at Barr City in Arapahoe County, Colorado, for only $10 an acre. Since the sojourner immigrant strategy was to make a quick nest egg and return to Italy, farming was clearly not for them. Few immigrants had the capital or the know-how needed to buy the equipment and supplies to establish a farm. Moreover, Italian immigrants moving to Chicago were part of a world-wide movement to escape the drudgery and isolation of farm life for the excitement of communal urban life.

Municipal (patronage and civil service) jobs are a good gauge of a group's successful integration into the power system. According to Humbert Nelli, 125 Italians worked as city street sweepers with others working as sewer diggers, asphalt helpers, and garbage collectors in 1895. Three Italians, Charles Arado (1884), Peter Raggio (1887), and Edward Martini (1891) were hired as police officers before 1900 and it is believed that Joseph Cassagrande in 1905 became the first Italian-American fireman. There followed a pattern of slow growth of Italian presence in the Chicago Police and Fire Departments. By 1915, 407 (73 males and 334 females) were employed as teachers by the Chicago Board of Education.

The 1911 Dillingham Report showed about 10 percent of their Italian sample as homeowners. Throughout the early twentieth century there continued to be a good deal of residential mobility among the Italians, as newcomers arrived and earlier immigrants bought homes in different zones. As with all immigrant groups, homeownership was a major goal.

What today would be called children or teenagers were also a source of income for the family. Before the 1920s, Italians were notorious among social workers and truant officers for keeping their children, especially girls, out of school. Young teen girls might take care of the house and the children, allowing the mother to work. Fourteen-year-old males on construction jobs were common. Almost universal was the experience of pre-teen boys hustling for cash. As Provenzano remembered:

> As a kid I remember going out shining shoes. I had a little box, and we used to go down along Blue Island Avenue and Halsted. We'd shine shoes, then I sold newspapers on Halsted and Adams. That's directly west from St. Peter's Church and the thing that I remember, we were getting there Sunday morning real early, to catch the parishioners as

> they come out to sell them their Sunday paper. We used to go what we call, junking, picking up, copper wire or rags and then we sold them for a few pennies.

As the density of Italian immigrants increased in a neighborhood, demand for traditional Italian products and services created a market for corner groceries, shoemaker shops, barber shops, bakeries, tailor shops, saloons, and undertakers. These small business ventures required a relatively small amount of capital and could often be staffed by the women and children of the family while the man of the house continued his day job. Others, like Agostino Boggiano and Giacomo Ucello, did the obvious. In 1880, they set up a macaroni factory that by 1917 became the largest in Chicago, employing 30 *paesani* and shipping the product nationwide. About 10 percent of Italians were listed by the Dillingham Report as being businessmen.

While the main theme of the immigration process is hard work, struggle, and slow progress, a small but significant number of Italian immigrants pushed their way onto the fast track. The beginnings of Italian migration to Chicago were marked by language confusion and hard work. Over time, the predominantly male work force began to sort itself out. Sojourners chose to return permanently and others, after various crossings, settled in the city as part of the chain migration that fueled the growth of a dozen Little Italies in the Chicago area.

Chapter Two

THE LITTLE ITALIES OF CHICAGO

There was never just one Little Italy in Chicago. If all Italian immigrants who came to Chicago had settled in the same neighborhood, the concentration of their political, economic, and cultural power would have produced a much different history. Because they came to work, they lived near their places of employment. They clustered in the "River Wards" in all three directions from the Loop. There were outlying colonies like Roseland, near the Pullman works, and there were Italian settlements in satellite suburbs like Chicago Heights. As chain migration proceeded, newcomers naturally headed to the neighborhood of their *paesani* and family, solidifying the dispersal of the Italian population in Chicago.

Though in its heyday, the Taylor Street area contained some 25,000 people—a third of the city's Italian population—there was from almost the beginning an absence of one large and densely populated Italian district. Into the 1920s people moved around a lot. In fact, no Chicago neighborhood was ever exclusively Italian. Following the pattern of ethnic succession, there were always remnants from previous ethnic populations, mixed with the current dominant ethnic populations, and a sprinkling of families from the ethnic group that might become the majority in a generation or two. Though the core Italian neighborhoods remained Italian, it was often different people who lived there, since earlier settlers were likely to have moved west to more desirable neighborhoods.

Typical chain migration patterns prevailed with families and villages gradually re-forming in Chicago neighborhoods as workers accumulated savings with which to send for their relatives and buy homes. Since the major colonies usually had a Catholic church as their focal center, a brief rundown of neighborhood/parish history offers a suitable structure for understanding the communal history of Chicago's Italians as they moved from immigrants to ethnics.

The original Genoese/Lucchese neighborhood, in the shadow of today's Merchandise Mart, produced the first Italian Catholic Church of the

Assumption in 1881, staffed by Servite priests. Father Sosteneus Moretti first built the basement foundation that was used as a place of worship until the fully completed church building was dedicated on the Feast of the Assumption, August 16, 1886. The generosity of the prominent Genovesi families and the artistic skills of Italian artisans made Assumption Church into a remarkable repository for devotional art. The splendid altar and spectacular stained glass windows were contributed by the Cuneo, Sbararo, and Lagorio families. As the first and only Italian Catholic Church in the city in its early years, Assumption claimed a congregation of 10,000. Father Tom Moreschini (pastor from 1893 to 1903) directed the building of the school in 1899. The Sisters of the Sacred Heart, led by their founder, Mother Frances X. Cabrini, ran the school. Though she traveled the world to carry on her mission, she spent considerable time in Chicago. In fact, it is reported that Mother Cabrini died on December 22, 1917, while preparing Christmas gifts for the children at Assumption School.

As the number of Italian parishes increased and commercial and industrial development pushed the population to the west, Assumption Church became more important as a symbolic shrine and "weekday church" for the faithful employees of the Merchandise Mart. Recently, the explosive growth of residential development in the River North area has again filled the pews of this venerable institution.

Perhaps Chicago's most colorful Italian sector was on the Near North Side. Known alternately as "Little Sicily" and "Little Hell," and featuring "Death Corner," this neighborhood was home to some 20,000 native-born Italians and Italian Americans by 1920. Most originated from the small towns surrounding Palermo, but there were also important contingents from Catania, Vizzini, and Sambuca-Zabat in eastern Sicily. According to Dr. Bruce Zummo, on Larabee Street there were many inhabitants from Altavilla Milicia. Those on Cambridge Avenue came from Chiusa and Caccamo. On Milton Avenue (now Cleveland Avenue) were the immigrants from Sambuca-Zabat. On Townsend Street resided families from Bagheria and Burgio. On North Cambridge Avenue, Hobbie Street, and Elm Street, the residents originated from the town of Corleone. The mix also included a sprinkling of so-called "Gai-gai" families—from Mezzoiuso—Albanian Sicilians from the Piana dei Greci. The Dillingham Commission reported only one northern Italian family, compared to 155 southern Italian families, in the Gault Court block of this area.

The Servite Church of St. Philip Benizi provided the backdrop for a score of patron saint street processions each summer sponsored by *paesani*-based mutual benefit societies. As related by Joe Camarda:

> The Feast in honor of the Blessed Mother took place at St. Philip Benizi Church on Oak Street and Cambridge Avenue extending to Larabee Street and Clybourn Avenue. I liked the way they used to decorate the street with festoons, banners, flags, illuminations—just like the old country. It lasted four days, always four days. The lodge's first building was in 1916. This was about a block away from the Church. There were food stands, rides and games and we always had the flying angels.

Sicilians from Bagheria celebrated the feast of St. Joseph, those from Ciminno honored the Crossifisso, and the Caccamesi honored Beato San Giovanni Liccio. Other Sicilian patron saints festivals that crowded the St. Philip's calendar were Santa Rosalia, San Nicola di Chiusa, the Immaculate Conception (Termini Imerese), Santissima Maria dell'Udienza (Sambuca), and San LeoLuca di Corleone. There was a street festival almost every summer Sunday.

Between 1904 and 1954, parish books at St. Philip's recorded 35,000 baptisms, 6,200 marriages, 12,000 confirmations, and 11,000 funerals. Since each of these 65,000 events represents a milestone in the life of an Italian individual and family, it is clear that the Church played an enormous role in this community.

The neighborhood was the focus of Harvey Zorbaugh's classic sociological study of 1929, *Gold Coast and Slum*. As he wrote:

> The extent to which family loyalty goes is almost beyond belief: no matter how disgraced or how disgraceful a member may be, he is never cast off; the unsuccessful are assisted; the selfish are indulged; the erratic patiently borne with. Old age is respected, and babies are objects of adoration.

The Near North neighborhood had the highest number of welfare cases in the city and welfare agencies considered Little Sicily the poorest neighborhood in Chicago. Yet Sicilian families in the area experienced almost no divorce and very little desertion.

Zorbaugh noted that even a moderately successful Sicilian in this neighborhood ran the risk of Black Hand extortion. The Black Hand was not an organization, but lawless individuals who sent blackmail letters and traded on the notorious reputation of the Mafia. The book took note of one Antonio Moreno, who broke the tradition and cooperated with police after his son was kidnapped. Though the perpetrators were arrested and convicted, they returned to the neighborhood a few months later to a rousing welcome from their friends and family.

From 1910 to 1930, within a half mile of the Sicilian neighborhood, there were about ten murders (usually unsolved) per year, with many of them taking place at the infamous "Death Corner" of Milton (Cleveland) and Oak Streets. Typically, the police blamed Italian killings on the Mafia and consoled themselves with the thought that they only kill each other anyway. On the other hand, residents were convinced all the police were on the take and that they were only making excuses for their corruption and/or their incompetence.

African-American residents began appearing in the neighborhood as early as the 1920s. Photos of the St. Joseph of Bagheria festivals in the 1930s show blacks and whites mixing. However, with the influx of African Americans to the area prior to World War II, and the decision by the FHA to build unsegregated public housing toward the western part of the neighborhood, Italian settlement on the north side faced a major challenge. Long time pastor Luigi Giambastiani used all his powers of persuasion both to slow down the rate of integration and to get the Italian community to buy into public housing units for themselves. It was through his efforts that the project bore the name of both an Illinois governor (Green) and the Italian saint who had lived in Chicago (Cabrini). He even spoke warmly at the groundbreaking ceremony in 1941 in hopes that Cabrini-Green would attract Italian tenants. His plan didn't work. Integration went forward and was quickened by the war; except at the beginning, public housing did not appeal to the relatively large Sicilian families; and, finally, when the Italian boys came back from the war, their ambition was to buy homes on the West Side or the Western Suburbs along Grand Avenue. Within the next 20 years whites fled the neighborhood, the project homes became overwhelmingly black, and the venerable Church of St. Philip Benizi was demolished to make way for more public housing.

Nearby to the west, an Italian community that included Sicilians and Pugliesi (Mola di Bari, Modugno, Ritigliano) and a smattering of immigrants from other parts of Italy, grew up around the Santa Maria Addolorata Parish. The first pastor, a certain Anthony D'Ercole, ran up a parish debt of $180,000 before Archbishop Quigley removed him and brought in the Scalabrinians Benjamin Franch (briefly) and then Father James Gambera. In his 17 years, Father Gambera successfully launched the parish community. Among his innovations were a nursery and kindergarten, which served 300 children, and evening classes in sewing and music. Apparently he was competing with the settlement houses in the area for the loyalty of the residents. The rough parish boundaries included the Italians from Ashland Avenue to the Chicago River, and from Hubbard Street to Chicago Avenue. Vecoli reported that the 1910 population of Italian ancestry in this 22nd Ward was 8,500. In 1924, Father Domenico Canestrini reported to Rome that the parish served 1,500 mostly large families of Sicilian and Baresi (Puglia) origin. He estimated the average Sunday attendance to be between 1,200 and 1,500. As of that year, the parish had no school but was in the process of purchasing land for one.

The most significant event in the life of this community came in the early morning hours of January 9, 1931, when a fire destroyed the church. The *Tribune* described the details:

> A spectacular fire early this morning swept through the Santa Maria Addolorata Catholic Church, on the south-west corner of Peoria Street and Grand Avenue, a Chicago landmark for 60 years. The fire caused a damage estimated at $125,000.00 by Fire Marshal Corrigan. Only the walls of the edifice were left standing. The glow of the fire was visible in the sky as far south as Roosevelt Road, and lighted the whole Italian district of the near North side.

The Fire Department Chaplain rescued the Blessed Sacrament from the flames while parishioners saw the flames gut the whole interior of the church. Though the building was grossly underinsured, the parish was able to continue by purchasing a Swedish Lutheran Church on the northwest corner of May and Erie Streets, which was refurbished and put into service as Addolorata Church until 1960 when yet another church building was erected.

Santa Maria Addolorata Church was the site of the first efforts at a Scalabrini Seminary in Chicago. Experience with the first half dozen seminarians at this location in the early 1930s convinced Father Franch and Father Pierini that there was enough support in the Italian community to expand the project and build the St. Charles Seminary in Stone Park.

The Como Inn, at Milwaukee near Grand, was opened by the Giuseppe Marchetti in 1924. For the next 80 years, the restaurant served as the venue for both the neighborhood and city-wide Italian market for wedding receptions and baptisms. Since it offered the hospitality of the Marchetti family, was convenient to downtown, and had free parking, the Como Inn became the unofficial home of Joint Civic Committee receptions and dinners.

Other important institutions in the neighborhood were the Vitucci Funeral home, Battista's Fish Store, Bari Foods, the Carpenter School, Vince's Barbershop, and the Near Northwest Side Civic Committee. Daniel "Moose" Brindisi was the moving force behind this delinquency prevention organization from the 1940s to the early 1990s. City fathers recognized Moose's lifetime of dedication by naming a stretch of Grand Avenue in his honor. His sons Caesar and Tim continue his work with youth. Still under the direction of the Scalabrini fathers, the Addolorata congregation is today a mixture of Italians, Hispanics, and yuppies. Though vestiges remain, the construction of the Kennedy Expressway and its ramps sliced up the neighborhood in the 1960s, undermining this once vibrant Sicilian/Barese neighborhood.

The Grand and Western Italian neighborhood grew up about a mile to the west of Addolorata and its residents worshiped at Holy Rosary Church. The 1910 population of Italians in the district was about 3,000. The Rago Funeral Home, Paterno's Pizza, and Armanetti's Liquor store were among the Italian institutions in the area. North of this was the Terra Cotta neighborhood, which was heavily populated by workers from the Northwestern Terra Cotta Company.

North Side Italians kept moving west along Grand Avenue and the 1990 census showed large numbers of them living in the Belmont-Craigin neighborhood, in the Grand and Harlem Avenue area, and in Elmwood Park. They brought many of their institutions with them, including the Maroons Soccer Club, Pompeo Stillo's Italian Tapes and Record Store, Gino Barsotti's Piazza Italia, and a host of restaurants and Italian coffee bars.

Toward the south end of the Loop, near Clark Street and the Polk Street Station, was the earliest colony of southern Italians. Vecoli lists the towns of origin of these settlers in the 1870s and 1880s as: Trivigno, Corleto, Calvello, and (especially) Laurenzana in Basilicata; Senarchia, Oliveto Citra, Teggiano, and (especially) Ricigliano in Campania; Cosenza, Rende, San Fili, and Fiumefreddo in Calabria. Starting in the 1870s, Luigi Spizziri reportedly induced hundreds from Potenza to settle along South Clark Street. Ricigliano reportedly lost half of its population in the wave of emigration that hit southern Italy at the end of the nineteenth century; most of those migrants came to Chicago. Men and boys from Ricigliano eventually monopolized the Loop area news vending stands and members of this group were legendary for pushing their children and grandchildren into the professions.

The 1910 Census showed nearly 5,000 persons of Italian ancestry on the Near South Side. Over the years the colony moved further south into what is now known as Chinatown, where they were joined by Sicilians from Nicosia. The Scalabrinian Church of Santa Maria Incoronata (patron saint of Ricigliano) remained the focal center for the community until the 1980s, when it became the Chinese mission of St. Theresa. The census showed 3,100 Italians in the Bridgeport neighborhood, especially in the Armour Square area just north of Comiskey Park.

This Halsted and Taylor Street area contained about 25,000 (1910), one-third, of the city's Italians—a mixture of people from Naples, Salerno, Bari, Messina, Palermo, Abruzzo, Calabria, Basilicata, the Marche, and Lucca. For many, this district served as a first settlement from which there was constant mobility. Though it was a very Italian area, it wasn't occupied by the same Italians year in and year out. Presumably the most fortunate moved west eight blocks to the Ashland Avenue neighborhood, making room for newcomers who were just starting out. Since the area was a multiethnic one, Italians shared the neighborhood with Russian Jews to the south and Greeks to the north. For the most part, this area was considered a slum in the pre-1920 era. Under the headline, "Foul Ewing Street: Italian Quarter that Invites Cholera and Other Diseases," a March 30, 1893 *Tribune* article described the scene:

> The street is lined with irregular rows of dinghy frame houses; innocent of paint and blackened and soiled by time and close contact with the children of Italy. The garbage boxes along the broken wood sidewalks are filled with ashes and rotting vegetables and are seldom emptied. Heaps of trash, rags, and old fruit are alongside the garbage boxes already overflowing. The dwelling houses and big tenement buildings that line Ewing Street are occupied by thousands of Italians. Every doorstep is well alive with children and babies dressed in rags and grime, many of their olive skinned faces showing sallow and wan beneath the covering of dirt. . . . Some of the dark complexioned

> men sit around tables through the day time hours and gamble at cards or dice with huge mugs of beer beside them.

From the time of its founding in 1888, Hull House had Italian immigrants as a major object of its reform agenda. The settlement house did mountains of research and writing to prove the obvious: wages were too low, housing conditions too crowded, municipal sanitary systems were inadequate, children needed more protection, political representatives of the area were corrupt, and so forth. More important, Hull House established a dizzying array of programs to help "settle" immigrants into their new society. The persuasive Ms. Addams also acted as a diplomat to Chicago's establishment and their wives. She was a champion fundraiser and was able to build Hull House into a 13-building complex that really made a difference in the lives of thousands of Italian immigrants. Moreover, Addams invented the profession of social work and was the role model for the international movement to use progressive efforts to improve the environment of the poor and offer them opportunities to acquire skills to make their own way in the world. The Chicago Commons and the Eli Bates House similarly served Italians on the North Side.

Unlike some of her successors in the field of social work, Jane Addams had a genuine love and respect for the culture of her clients. Working closely with Alessandro Mastro-Valerio, the editor of *La Tribuna Transatlantica*, Hull House frequently scheduled "Italian Nights" with appropriate music and food to celebrate Italian heroes like Garibaldi and Mazzini. While Hull House was basically run by "do-gooding outsiders," its system of organizing self-governing clubs to pursue various interests and hobbies did instill a strong degree of indigenous leadership in the participants.

Jane Addams had her limitations. In her early years, Addams imagined that she could displace the obviously corrupt machine politicians in her area and even ran for alderman, but she learned that her adversaries had a "social work" system of their own. Alderman John Powers was not Italian, but he called himself Gianni di Paoli and used his influence to get Italians jobs on the city clean up crews, deliver coal to the needy in the dead of winter, and get Italian boys out of scrapes with the law. He attended every wake and at election time he did the rounds at the saloons and bought the *paesani* beers. How could Jane Addams match that?

The Catholic Church's response to the Italian situation in the neighborhood resulted in the founding of the Holy Guardian Angel parish in the 1890s. A

Jesuit teacher at St. Ignatius High School, Father Paolo Ponsilione, took it upon himself to work with Italians in the area who found that Assumption Italian Catholic Church was too far away and because they felt unwelcome at the nearby Irish churches. Father Edmund Dunne, S.J., known as *Zi' Prete* (Uncle Priest), took up the task by officially establishing the parish in 1898. The next year, Dunne built a church on Arthington Street, then two years later a rectory building and addition to the church before he was elected Bishop of Peoria. At this point Archbishop Quigley entrusted the parish, Holy Guardian Angel (*Sant'Angelo Cusode*) to his friend, Pacifico Chenuil, thus creating in 1903 the first Scalabrini parish in Chicago. Weekly attendance was high. Serving an estimated 20,000 Italians in 5,000 families, the church averaged around 1,200 baptisms and 160 weddings a year from 1903 to 1911. After a good deal of foot-dragging, the parish opened its school in 1920. Family membership fell to just 500 in 1947 because of neighborhood changes in both land use and population. In an effort to revitalize the parish, Father Italo Scola led a campaign to build a new combination church/school in the late 1950s. Shortly after the project was completed, the city of Chicago embarked on building the Dan Ryan Expressway and the University of Illinois. Since the church was apparently located in the path of the expressway and since the neighborhood served by the church was slated for demolition, Guardian Angel was dissolved in 1960.

The commercial center of this Little Italy was at the intersection of Taylor and Halsted Streets, just a few blocks north of the Maxwell Street Market. Taylor and Halsted was the "Italian Downtown." Over the years in this shopping district you could find the Conte di Savoia Food Store, Lezza's Pastries, Serafina Ferrara's (wedding cake) Bakery, Chicago Spices, Bragno wines and liquors, the Chesrow Drugstore, Edoardo Colombo's Italian American Radio Programming, Sam Del Vecchio's Grocery, Undertaker David Piegare, Cillel and Son marble works, Salvino-Personeni Pharmacy, De Cristofaro and Cambio grocery, the Nuti Bakery, Carlo Fillipelli's Grocery, Umberto Sarno's candy company, and the Banco di Napoli.

In its heyday, the Guardian Angel parish grew so quickly that an additional Italian church, Our Lady of Pompeii (OLP), was established just a few blocks west on Lexington at McAllister Street. The church opened its doors in early April 1911 with Father Chenuil's assistant, Father Peter Barabino, as it pastor. The early parish boasted a church/school combination facility and proceeded on a lengthy campaign to continue to build the requisite physical plant consisting of church-school, convent, rectory, new church, and expanded school as the Italian population in the area continued to rise. When the current church building was erected in 1924 in the pastorship of Father Carlo Fani, the project was blessed with a gift from the estate of Alderman John Powers of $12,000 for the splendid white marble altar.

In the Depression Era, Father Remigio Pigato worked to form the OLP Mothers' Guild and reactivate the Saint Vincent de Paul Society to combat the poverty and unemployment among parishioners. It was also during this period that the church developed a cooperative arrangement with the Near West Side Community Committee (NWSCC). Led by the young Anthony Sorrentino, this group was based on the philosophy of University of Chicago sociologist Clifford Shaw. Contrary to the Jane Addams social work model, Shaw believed that social change would best take place through self-help and that the problems of the immigrants would best be solved by indigenous leaders, like Sorrentino, who had a better chance of being taken seriously by "risk" youth. Shaw's Chicago Area Project (CAP) provided some funding and Sorrentino was eventually able to win support from religious leaders, businessmen, and political figures from the area such as Paul D'Arco, Reverend Remigio Pigato, Sam Serpe, John Romano, Joseph Guinta, Louis Di Fonso, Luigi Rovai, Reno Alghini, Ralph Argento, Fred D'Angelo, Emil Peluso (who later became the organization's president and executive director), Judge Peter R. Scalise (retired), Dr. Vito R. Lucatorto (retired), Joseph Rovai, Ernest Mategrano Sr., Ernest Mategrano Jr., Anthony De Raffaele, Pat De Mario, Carmen Carsello, Nick A. Taccio, James Serpe, Louis Lonigro, John Giampa, and many others.

A major project of the NWSCC was the creation of Camp Pompeii in what is now University Park. As the *Tribune* described the camp in 1942:

> Now there is a neat little farmhouse on Monee road, just south of the Sauk Trail four miles west of Chicago Heights. Past the Farm house a narrow road winds back into the woods. There in a clearing, is the mess hall—nothing more nor less than two old portable school buildings joined as one large structure. It cost the West Side Community council, 1035 Polk street, sponsoring agency, more to move the buildings out to the camp than It did to purchase them, but even so the cost was small.

In the 60 years since it was established, thousands of urban kids have benefited from its sports and recreational opportunities. A similar indigenous neighborhood club from the Northwest Side was managed for many years by Moose Brindisi.

On the fiftieth anniversary of the parish, the commemorative booklet reported that Our Lady of Pompeii Church baptized 28,000 children, extended First Communion and confirmation to 17,500, married 7,150 couples, and buried 9,100. The second 50 years in the history of OLP proved more troublesome as the University of Illinois in the 1960s replaced the homes of thousands of its parishioners. Enrollment dropped to such a point at the school that it was closed and eventually the Scalabrini Fathers gave up their interest in the facility. To avoid closing the church, a group rallied around OLP to designate it as a shrine to serve Italians throughout the city. Father Richard Fragomeni for the past decade has presided over a lively Italian-oriented liturgical program and other community boosters like Paula and Oscar D'Angelo and Joe Gentile have done fundraising to maintain the physical plant. In keeping with tradition, Columbus Day festivities begin at Our Lady of Pompeii. The Scalabrini priests also controlled St. Collistus Church a few blocks to the west of Pompeii Church, which ministered to the flow of the Italian population going in that direction.

In addition to these major inner-city Italian enclaves, a number of outlying colonies formed in the pre-1920 period. Closest in was the settlement of Toscani at 24th and Oakley where many worked at the McCormick Reaper plant. They came from Ponte Buggianese, Bagni di Lucca, Montecatini, and other small towns near the ancient fortified city of Lucca in the Tuscany Region of Northern Italy. The Dillingham Commission showed 67 northern Italian families and only one southern Italian family in a two-block sample of this neighborhoods. Historically socialist in politics and virtually crime-free, the population was much smaller than other Italian zones.

Sociologist Peter Venturelli, who has written a dissertation and several articles about his home neighborhood, documented the population at a steady 1,200 in the period from the 1890s to 1981. Unlike the Near West and North Side Italian neighborhoods, there was not much turnover in the population; urban renewal and white flight did not uproot the community. However, a coterie of National Melleable employees in 1910 followed their jobs a few miles west when Melleable opened its Grant Works in Cicero. Reportedly, their new neighborhood was replete with amenities but had no church, nor did they want one.

Over the past few decades the Oakley Italian population has dwindled and many have relocated in suburban Addison. Yet, for a century, the compact character of the neighborhood brought together many ethnic institutions that reinforced each other and make Oakley, today, perhaps the best preserved Little Italy in the city. Still functioning within a few blocks of each other are St. Michael the Archangel Church, the Po Piedmonte Club, a funeral home, bakery, barbershop, and several Tuscan Italian restaurants and groceries. The physical and social closeness of the community resulted in greater retention of the Italian language in Oakley than in other immigrant neighborhoods. This ambience is what makes the Oakley neighborhood ideal as the location for the annual "Heart of Italy" festival that has taken place here since the late 1990s.

In the early years, St. Michael the Archangel (patron saint of Lucca) Church had a difficult time asserting its leadership. For many years after the church was established in 1903, St. Michael was faced with an effective socialist campaign "to free men from the slavery of religion." This campaign thwarted the efforts of a rapid succession of earnest and hard-working Scalabrinians. As Eddie Baldacci remembered it:

> In the early days, sometimes people would try and harass the people going to church. They might harass them if they were maybe talking, around the corner. "Are you gonna go to *church*?" Maybe something like that. "You stupid individual." Oh yes, I can visualize that . . . because Nello, this guitar player that was like my second father, he was dead set against the church.

Eventually radicalism diminished and by the 1950s Father Louis Donanzan was able to win the cooperation of former adversaries, finally build a school for St. Michael's, and erase the parish debt.

At 67th Street and Hermitage and in the Grand Crossing area were two settlements of migrants from Salerno and Calabria respectively. St. Mary of Mount Carmel served the former. The Hermitage settlement traced its origins back to 1888 when railroad workers from Oliveto Citra (Salerno) realized the possibilities of this sparsely populated mid-southwest zone. They decided to move out of the slum conditions on South Clark Street and return to the kind of rural environment they knew as *contadini* without having to give up their railroad jobs. While Italian immigrants mostly resisted the blandishments by reformers to get them to go into farming full time, they still possessed the urge to grow things. They possessed gardening skills and they could feed their families abundantly with the fruit and vegetables they could grow, not to mention the more convenient wine making that could take place in the wide open spaces around 67th Street. Vecoli tells how they purchased land at bargain prices, built wooden shacks, and in a few years converted the prairie land into verdant gardens. By 1910, over 1,000 Italians lived there, including immigrants from Contursi, Campagna, and Sanarchia. They kept so many goats that people called the zone "Goatsville." The errant behavior by some of the goats on neighbors' property often got their owners into trouble with the police.

From the beginning, the Olivetani celebrated the feast of Our Lady of Mount Carmel (OLMC) and the event had a similar impact as the OLMC event had on Melrose Park: it attracted new Italian residents to the district. In 1903, barber Paul Carelli also spearheaded the celebration of the Feast of San Rocco di Potenza Lucania, which continued to be observed at St. Mary of Mount Carmel into the 1960s when white residents began moving out of this part of the South Side. Due in no small part to the efforts of a Sears executive, Leonard Giuliano and his family, the feast continues to this day. It was most recently celebrated at St. William Church on the city's northwest side.

Also to the south, in the famous planned-company town established by and named after George Pullman, there was a colony of Italian brickmakers and others from the Altopiano Asiago area of the Veneto region. The nearby Roseland neighborhood was also home to a contingent of Piedmontese and Sicilians. The Scalabrinian Church of St. Anthony of Padua (1906) served this group. About 1,600 Italian-born residents were reported in this part of the city in 1920. Second and third generation offspring multiplied those numbers significantly. In the next 70 years, the church presided over 11,120 baptisms, 8,060 First Communions, 3,922 weddings, 4,782 burials, and 2,400 eighth-grade graduations. Culturally, Roseland was probably the most exciting Italian neighborhood. Mario Manzardo described the scene in a 1973 newspaper article:

> The Giovanni Bartoli Music School was flowering: Antonio Zordan, Agusto Dalle Molle, and Peter Toniazzo were emerging as some of the new talented musicians in the area. A popular military band held weekly practice in the back of Gasperini's shoe repair shop and another band that later became known as the *Bell'Italia* Band, were much in demand for concerts and local parades. . . . Often on weekends there was cabaret entertainment for families . . . singers

> would sing the romantic Italian songs of Paolo Tosti and Enrico Toselli, as well as operatic arias.

The Roseland Operetta Club also provided a steady diet of high Italian culture to large and appreciative audiences. Amabile Santacaterina (later known as "Mrs. Belgo" for her Italian frozen foods) was only one of dozens of people in the Roseland area who actively participated in the elaborate stagings of the Operetta Club. In the 1930s, they had a lot of time to devote to the musical productions because almost everyone was out of work. She later became one of the many Italian language radio personalities who promoted the building of the Villa Scalabrini.

Roseland was the best organized Italian community in Chicago. The greater Roseland area boasted more than its share of mutual benefit societies, including the San Luigi di Tresche Conca, Cesuna, Caltranese, San Alessandro Del Caretto, and the Piedmontese societies, as well as the Unione Veneziana, the Anita Garibaldi, Tito Schipa, Umberto I, and the Roma Lodge. And that doesn't include a dozen or so church societies or the various socialist organizations.

Most impressive of the Roseland voluntary organizations was the staff of the St. Anthony *Broadcast.* During World War II this group assiduously put together news of all the Roseland boys in the service. They got the addresses of each of the men, solicited information about them directly and through relatives, and put out a monthly newsletter to hundreds of people stationed all over the world. The *Broadcast* contributed mightily to Roseland's strong sense of community in the post war era by reinforcing the soldiers' identities as Roselandites and as Americans.

In the post-war period, the people of Roseland were confident about their future; employment was high, the stores on commercial streets were doing good business, and membership at St. Anthony Church reached 2,500 families with 700 students in the school. In 1959, ground was broken for a new church building. Opened in 1961, the new St. Anthony of Padua Church had an interior that resembled a basilica. Then came an expansion of the African-American community that encompassed almost all of the South Side. At the same time, St. Anthony began attracting Mexican-American worshippers.

Just 15 years after the dedication of the new church, Carmen Adducci suggested to her readers in the *70th Anniversary Booklet* that the church would persevere with its mission to help immigrants whether they spoke Italian or Spanish. In any case, the dynamics of blockbusting, panic peddling, and white flight kicked in with a vengeance, dispersing Roseland Italians to Chicago Heights, Lansing, and points south. Others ended up in the western suburbs.

Melrose Park, 16 miles west of the central city, was a place of second settlement attracting Riciglianesi ("Richies"), Trivignesi ("Trivies"), and others from the inner city to the wide open spaces of the western suburbs. Gabriel and Leonard DeFranco (from Castiglione, Abruzzi) were the first Italians to settle in Melrose (1888). They established a barbershop/cigar store/real estate business and Leonard emerged in 1903 as the first Italian Village Board member in 1903.

The Melrose Park Italian community owes its existence to Our Lady of Mount Carmel. Emanuella De Stefano, a native of the town of Laurenzana (Potenza), prayed to Our Lady of Mount Carmel for the life of her gravely ill husband, Emilio De Stefano, the well-known leader of the Laurenzanesi community. He recovered. In gratitude, Emanuella and her friend, Anna Marie Prignano, organized in July of 1894 the first Festa Della Madonna in Melrose Park on the De Stefano farm on 25th Avenue at North Avenue. The mass was presided over by Father Thomas Moreschine, the pastor at Assumption Church.

The rest is history. The tradition has entered its second century. More than a million people have at one time or another attended the Feast of Our Lady of Mount Carmel. In the early years, increased numbers of inner-city Italians attended the feast and liked the gardening possibilities (the Melrose Pepper) presented by the rural atmosphere of Melrose. The De Stefanos urged them to come live in Melrose Park. The parish grew along with the Italian population. The faithful pressed for a church for Our Lady of Mount Carmel, and finally in 1905, the Scalabrini Order sent Father Benjamin Franch to lead the congregation to a new church in 1906 and a school in 1913. He stayed for 50 years.

Melrose Park became identified as the quintessential Italian suburb in the Chicago area. Italians dominated the politics of Proviso Township and at one point were successful in controlling the board at Triton College. Melrose Park remains the town shaped by devotion to Our Lady of Mount Carmel. This Italian identity is so strong that it will, no doubt, endure even the demographic change that is making the Melrose Park population more Hispanic than Italian.

The town of Blue Island at the southwest border of the city was heavily settled by Italian railroad workers from Potenza, Melfi, Avigliano, and some from Cosenza and Catanzaro, but mostly from Ripacandida (Basilicata) who had first migrated to Altoona, Pennsylvania. In 1905, they formed the Society of San Donato, martyred patron saint of Ripacandida, in hopes of founding an Italian Catholic Church in Blue Island. Within a few years, their hopes were realized and a sizable settlement grew up around the St. Donatus Church north of 127th Street east of the Rock Island Railroad tracks. The church was not staffed by the Scalabrini Fathers. The concentration of Italians was great enough to elect Italians as aldermen beginning in 1919 and extending into the 1980s, when one of their own, John Rita, was elected mayor. Though there has been movement of Italians away from Blue Island, the August Feast of San Donatus maintains some flavor of *Italianitá* in the town.

Chicago Heights, 30 miles to the south of the Loop and a satellite suburb similar to Blue Island, had a population of 20,000 with 50 percent Italian stock by 1920. For most, it was a place of first settlement. The majority were Marchigiani, hailing from San Benedetto del Tronto and nearby towns. They made up about 60 percent of the Italian population. Each contributed about ten percent of the Italian population in Chicago Heights from Amaseno (Frosinone), the Sicilian town of Caccamo near Termini Imerese. Many of the latter came by way of New Orleans. Castel di Sangro (Abruzzi) also contributed a good number of immigrants to Chicago Heights.

The wave of Italian immigration coincided perfectly with the rapid expansion of heavy industry in Chicago Heights, and the Italian colony prospered along with the industries. During the Prohibition Era, several Sicilian bootleggers developed connections with Al Capone and the town gained some notoriety for well-publicized beer barrel busting raids by federal agents.

Their church, San Rocco, was founded in 1906 by Father Pasquale Renzullo. Renzullo remained pastor until 1922 and had to battle apathy, anti-clerical outbursts by Italian socialists, and competition from the Presbyterian Italian mission, the Church of Our Savior. Despite setbacks, however, the pastor succeeded in establishing the Mount Carmel School in 1912, staffed by the Sisters of St. Joseph. Also high on the agenda was the Athletic Club in 1919, and institutions that played an important role in the community for years to come. The school taught some Italian, and the Mount Carmel athletic club taught leadership and discipline, also providing an entree for Italian youth into the very important amateur sports scene in Chicago Heights.

The Italian community maintains an active sister city relationship between Chicago Heights and San Benedetto del Tronto. The Societá Amaseno, revitalized by a post–World War II migration, stages the very successful Feast of San Lorenzo each August. Over time Italians became the most important ethnic group in the city, dominating local politics in the last half of the twentieth century, even though their percentage of the population has been steadily dwindling. For a full discussion of Italians in Chicago Heights, consult the author's website at http://www.ecnet.net/users/gcandel/home.html.

The Highwood community, 28 miles north of the Loop, developed after the turn of the century when migrants from the Modenese towns of Sant'Anna Peligo and Pievepeligo settled there after venturing into the coal mining towns of downstate Illinois. As explained by Adria Bernardi in her *Houses with Names*, they made their way in the world "working for some rich people" doing landscaping (Donald Bernardi, Tins Pedruci, Angelo Gualandri) and housekeeping for North Shore business leaders. Highwood artisans and their brethren throughout the Chicago area gained early prominence in the marble and stone carving business. Antonio Ferrarini's Italian Marble Company, Alfred Galassini's National Marble, Peter Lamberti's monument statuary work, the Fabbri and Fiocchi stone carving firms, and the leadership of the Marble Setters Union (Peter Zini) represent the artistic role played by Italian workers in creating the beauty and grace of public buildings, churches, and homes in the city.

Since most nearby towns on the North Shore are wealthy residential suburbs with very restrictive zoning and liquor laws, soldiers and sailors from the nearby Ft. Sheridan and Great Lakes Naval Base often sought out restaurants and bars in Highwood. The town is known for its fine Italian eateries, which include the venerable Del Rio—run for three generations by the Pigato family.

Into the 1980s there were a large number of recent arrivals and it was common to hear Italian spoken on the street of Highwood. Father Joseph Currielli, the pastor of St. James Church, estimated in that year half of his parishioners were bilingual.

The Bocce Club of Highwood is world class. Its dozen top-notch indoor courts make it possible to host national bocce tournaments and sponsor its own Silver Cup competition each November. The Club carries on a long Highwood tradition of women's bocce, which was pioneered by the 500-member Italian Women's Prosperity Club and its longtime president, Mary Somenzi.

Another community in Chicago usually not mentioned as an Italian area is a West Side neighborhood near Chicago Avenue and Pulaski with no special name. Originally Irish, this was a blue collar neighborhood of second settlement for second generation Italians who made up about 60 percent of the residents, with about 30 percent Irish and the rest of Polish and Eastern European ancestry. Italians owned many of the small shops along Chicago Avenue near Kedzie. The neighborhood Catholic church was Our Lady of the Angels. The parish included 4,500 registered families and was one of the largest and most thriving parishes in the archdiocese. Masses and confessions were done in both English and Italian. Two of the seven priests, Joseph Ognibene and Alfred Corbo, were Italian.

A little after 2:30 p.m. on December 1, 1958, their world fell apart when a fire swept through Our Lady of the Angels School, killing 88 students and 3 nuns. Another 90 students and 3 nuns were seriously injured. Several injured children subsequently died, bringing the death toll to 95. In such a disaster, ethnicity loses relevance. Yet the fact is that 40 of the children killed in the fire bore Italian names. The 1,200 students attending the school and their families were traumatized by the catastrophe and the event effectively killed the neighborhood.

There was no one Little Italy and there was no one town or region of origin that defined the world Italian immigrants made during the past century. The pattern that emerges is a varied one. Though merchants came first, mostly *contadini* (small farmers) from scores of towns in Italy, both north and south, settled around the core of the central city and selected suburbs. They practiced *campanilismo*, living near others from the same village or region. The inner-city colonies were considered slums, and their inhabitants were the object of intensive efforts by social workers to make them middle class. Political ward bosses wanted their votes and the Church wanted to save their immortal souls. And they had their own ideas about how to advance their families.

Though the Italian communities had a lot in common, each colony developed and changed at its own pace, depending on its geographic location and the dynamic mix of Italians and other immigrants who lived in them. Their world was not a static one. Most of the neighborhoods lasted pretty much intact until about 1960 when the roof literally fell in. The pressures of urban life mangled or completely destroyed many of the churches and the neighborhoods and community networks they had built. With the demise of St. Philip Benizi, Holy Guardian Angel, Our Lady of Mount Carmel, Santa Maria Incoronata, Our Lady of the Angels, and the Italian communities they represent, we are left with very little physical evidence of the Italian immigrant presence in Chicago. The Pompeii Shrine and parts of the Near West Side, the 24th and Oakley area, and the Assumption Church survive as the only material links (within the city limits) to the world the Italian immigrants made and the lives that they lived.

Chapter Three

IMAGES AND IMPRESSIONS OF ITALIAN CHICAGO

Image is important. Italian culture worships the concept of *La Bella Figura.* Gloria Nardini has written a book with that phrase as the title. Her subject is an Italian women's club and the emphasis they put on making a good show. The major contemporary issue for Chicago Italian Americans is the negative media image from which they suffer.

While part of this problem is directly traceable to the Al Capone gangster days, we often ignore the images and self-images held by and about Italians in Chicago in the pre-Capone days. The city had numerous Italian language newspapers in the period before World War II, and the various metropolitan newspapers also made mention of some people and events in the Italian community. Aside from the narrative of events and accomplishments in the Italian community, we can get a feel for immigrant life through a sample survey of the media of the day—newspapers.

Humbert Nelli's 1965 study of the Italian language press listed 26 newspapers that served Chicago readers for varying lengths of time. *L'Unione Italiana* was the first to appear in 1867, surviving under a different name only until 1869. In the period before 1920, almost half of the publications listed were socialist organs of one type or another. *La Fioccola* (1912–1921) and *Vita Nuova* were Protestant publications. However, *L'Italia* (1886–1963) and *La Tribuna Transatlantica* (1898–1924) emerge as the major Italian newspapers of their era. Since literacy rates among Italian immigrants were abysmal, the impact of Italian language newspapers is problematic. On the other hand, friends could read the newspapers to those who were not literate. Moreover, one could argue that *L'Italia* and other Italian publications reached and influenced the thinking of the "leadership class." In any case, the back issues of these publications are fascinating documents that preserve many long-forgotten events and personalities. They provide convincing evidence of the manner in which Italians were regarded and the manner in which they, themselves, wished to be regarded.

Oscar Durante, a native of Naples, started *L'Italia* as a teenager in 1886 and made the publication into an enduring institution second in importance only to Generoso Pope's *Il Progresso*, which had the advantage of the larger New York base. In its early years, *L'Italia* established itself as the Italian paper with America's largest circulation (17,000 in the early 1890s). Distribution reached 30,000 in 1915 and 38,000 in 1921. In the 1920s, Durante's publication lost the national competition but continued to be the top seller in Chicago and the West. Ricilianesi news vendors hawked *L'Italia* at newsstands throughout the Loop. Since the Italian population in Chicago was estimated at 100,000 during that period, *L'Italia* apparently ended up in the hands of one out of every ten Italians in the city. It started as a weekly and in 1913 switched to publication three times a week in tabloid form.

L'Italia was a mainstream publication loyal to the Republican Party, Americanization, and what would today be called middle class values. A staunch protector of Italian immigrants, the paper was nevertheless disturbed and embarrassed by the presence of Italian ragpickers. Durante supported local ordinances against the practice even while claiming that the English language press exaggerated the negative stories about Italian ragpickers. Durante deplored the conditions in the Italian slums, but pointed out that you don't have to be Italian to live in a slum—plenty of American and non-Italian neighborhoods had similar situations to the ones (over)reported in the daily press.

The editor was irritated by many of the practices of lower class Italian women and berated them for baring their breasts and nursing their babies in public. He was also upset about the dirty and unkempt appearance of many Italian laborers, the practice of 30-year-old men marrying teenagers, and the desire of Italian parents to put their kids to work at the earliest possible age, depriving them of a decent education. Even though the newspaper was published in Italian, it continually crusaded for Italians to learn English, attend night school, and become United States citizens as quickly as possible.

Of course, *L'Italia* was in the forefront in decrying the injustice of the New Orleans lynching of 11 Sicilians in 1890. The paper blamed the white establishment for its prejudice against Italians and denied the existence of a "mafia" organization. *L'Italia* publicized events in the Italian community such as the *Societá di C. Colombo* (of which the editor was a member), the *Societá Italiane Unite* dance, and the results of the Corte Italia 68 election.

L'Italia protested the use of the term "Dago" in an 1886 *Chicago Tribune* story. In an unusual English language editorial, Durante used dignity and restraint in pointing out that "anyone pretending to be a gentleman" would never use such a word. And since the *Tribune* had the "high mission" to represent American public opinion, it should not apply terms to Italians which they consider to be a gross insult.

L'Italia also regularly reminded Italians in America of the September 22 anniversary of Italian unification and Garibaldi's birthday, and the scheduled festivities to honor these Italian holidays. The newspaper office even acted as a postal address and *L'Italia* regularly printed the names of people for whom it had received mail. This must have been an important service for the itinerant workers on railroad gangs and others who changed their address frequently. The paper promoted fundraising campaigns to erect statues and monuments to Italian heroes in Chicago Parks and for the relief of victims of earthquakes in Italy. Schiavo gives Durante credit for getting the city of Chicago to name Columbus Drive and Giuseppe Verdi School after Italian heroes.

Sympathetic profiles of Italian-American achievers in *L'Italia* helped to build up the reputations of successful Italian leaders, businessmen, and mainstream political figures (mostly Republican). On various occasions the newspaper celebrated the community's lawyers, physicians, manufacturers, and businessmen with proud lists and profiles of super achievers.

Though Republican in philosophy, *L'Italia* implored Italian workers not to act as scabs or strikebreakers. The paper supported the unsuccessful Hart, Schaffner, and Marx strike of 1910. And in 1909 it deplored the fact that the old line wealthy Italians had not financed more institutions like schools and hospitals to help the poor immigrants from the south of Italy.

Durante was such a strong supporter of national unity in Italy in the 1890s that he characterized the Pope in that era as the "relentless enemy of our unity." But later he also criticized the Italian government for not protecting Italian immigrants more effectively, claiming that the government was only interested in the positive economic impact in Italy of remittances that the immigrants sent back. While Durante supported the Italian cause in World War I, he was critical of the country's efforts to recruit immigrants to return to Italy to fight in the Italian Army. He supported the United States' entry into the war and urged Italian Americans to buy war bonds and answer the draft. Along with most Italians in America, Durante lost confidence in President Wilson when the treaty ending the war failed to award Trieste to Italy. *L'Italia* supported Mussolini's rise to power in the early 1920s. In various forms *L'Italia* lived on until the 1950s.

Another Italian language Chicago newspaper of note was *La Tribuna Transatlantica*. Alessandro Mastro-Valerio and Giuseppi Ronga established the publication in 1898. The former served as the editor and publisher from 1898 to 1924. He was an outspoken liberal reformer and a close ally of Jane Addams. A Hull House admirer called him a "Chicago Garibaldi who is trying to lead the Italians out of the bondage of ignorance."

The focus of *La Tribuna* was much more local and literary than that of *L'Italia*. Mastro-Valerio led the campaign to remove John Powers as alderman of the 19th Ward, supported the garment strikers, and aided the formation of a "White Hand Society" to combat the wave of Black Hand extortion and kidnappings that plagued the immigrant community. He was a strong advocate of a spectacularly unsuccessful back-to-the-land movement for Chicago *paesani*. The newspaper did battle with both the Irish-dominated Roman Catholic hierarchy and with the folk religion of his *paesani*. Mastro-Valerio was one of those Italians who was offended by patron saint celebrations. Writing in August 1905, he took exception to the excesses of the Our Lady of Mount Carmel celebration in Melrose Park, attended by 10,000. For Mastro-Valerio, parading a graven image through the streets and pinning money to the image amounted to fanaticism and superstition. He found it a disgrace and referred to the lay organizers as "racketeers." Moreover, the $800 pinned to the Virgin's robe should have gone to feed starving Italian families.

Most of the Italian publications were run by nationalists like Mastro-Valerio, the socialists (*La Parola del Popolo*, *La Parola dei Socialisti*, etc.) and the Protestants (the Presbyterian *La Vita Nuova* and the Methodist *La Fioccola*). Before the advent of the *Fra Noi* in 1960, the printed word in the Italian media was mostly anti-Catholic.

In later years the masthead of *La Tribuna Transatlantica* featured a map of the Atlantic Ocean with Columbus's three ships heading for America with fish jumping from the waters. In March 1919, the headline protested the coming of Prohibition with the headline "NO WINE, NO WORK" and went on to argue that Italians must suffer because others (Irish?) abuse alcohol, that the measure was passed into law insidiously and that Prohibition would simply convince good Italians to return to the Old Country.

Chicago's Italian community also included a cohort of socialists, loosely affiliated with the American Socialist Party. They had a great deal of credibility before World War I and the Bolshevik Revolution made socialism tantamount to treason. The fascinating saga of Chicago's Italian socialists has been captured in *Struggling in Chicago: Italian Immigrants with a Socialist Agenda, 1880–1980*, written by Eugene Miller and Gianna Sommi Panofsky, which is (lamentably) unpublished as of this writing.

Italian language publications played a key role in their efforts as radicals sought to educate and organize the Italian working class. Under the leadership of Giuseppe Bertelli and his *La Parola dei Socialisti*, founded in 1908, a significant group supported the labor movement and fought fascism. Some elements of the group even survived into the 1980s thanks to Egidio Clemente's valiant efforts to keep the socialist spirit alive via *La Parola del Popolo*.

Because of the language diversity of American workers, the Socialist Party of America was divided into ethnic sections and nationally the Italian Socialist Federation was one of the most important. In the last decades of the nineteenth century the Italian government put a great deal of pressure on socialist and radical elements, causing them to flee to places like Chicago. After 1900, Chicago was a union town and many of the union members and leaders were socialist. Since Chicago was the rail capital of the nation, the socialists and the radical unionists like the Industrial Workers of the World used Chicago as a base to organize workers in the West, especially miners. There was also a good deal of radical activity in the Spring Valley area and in other coal mining towns of Illinois.

La Parola and the other socialist publications projected an image of Italian workers as oppressed immigrants. Along with immigrants of other nationalities, Italians should organize in various unions to bring economic justice to capitalist America. The movement focused on the need for long term education on economic issues to raise the awareness of the workers and create class consciousness.

In a bewildering odyssey of crises and ideological disputes, the Italian socialist movement in Chicago was buffeted by the suppression of their publications during World War I and the split between the Communists and the Socialists resulting from the Russian Revolution. Then came the Red Scare and the Palmer Raids of 1920 and the deportation of suspected radicals. Socialists also disagreed over the unfair handling of Italy's claims to Trieste in the Versailles Treaty. The mood of America in the 1920s was very anti-radical, and the Sacco and Vanzetti trials ended after seven years in the numbing reality of their execution.

In this same period, socialists took on their struggle with Mussolini's fascist regime in both Italy and America. In the 1930s, they also became involved with the Congress of Industrial Organizations (CIO) in organizing the bread delivery men, and finally in the 1940s they got their opportunity to aid American forces in military conquest of fascist Italy. Bertelli, and then Clemente, as the editor of Italian Socialist publications over seven decades, chronicled the ebb and flow of the dwindling movement in Chicago. Egidio Clemente's story, as told in *Voices of America: Italians in Chicago*, colorfully recounts this dramatic tale.

In a period when literacy rates were much lower than they are today, photos in the mainstream newspapers played an important role in developing the image and self-image of Chicago's Italians. An Internet search of the *Chicago Daily News* Photo Archives from 1902 to 1933 in the Chicago Historical Society (at http://memory.loc.gov) reveals that the newspaper collected and possibly published a wide variety of images relating to Italians in that time period.

The photos include events of the era, personalities, street scenes, Black Hand Crime, and bootleg era gangsters. Most worthy of mention are: photos depicting the Cherry (Illinois) mine disaster that killed 250 (mostly Italian) miners in 1908; the 1920 tornado that hit Melrose Park; the arrest of Northwestern student Aurora D'Angelo for leading a disturbance following the execution of Sacco and Vanzetti in 1927; and the funeral of murdered politician/gangster Diamond Joe Esposito (1928). There were photos of visiting Italian nobility, Italian Ambassador Baron DesPlanches (1908), opera stars like Enrico Caruso (1920) and musical director of the Chicago Opera, Cleofonte Campanini (1914), and orchestra conductor Giorgio Polacco (1928). A goodwill visit by Italian soldiers and General Diaz apparently to recruit immigrants for the Italian Army also merited a photo session in 1915.

Most interesting for a glimpse into the lives of immigrants in the neighborhood are the photos of Dr. Annie Carlo Basi, known as the Queen of Little Italy. Having the appearance of the "Lady in the Big Fat Purse," Dr. Basi is shown with her doctor's satchel on a commercial street surrounded by admiring prospective patients. Also among the photos are images of the victims of Black Hand bombings such as the Joseph Carsello family of 846 S. Miller Street (1913) and Angelo Marino of 852 Gault Court (1911) and accused Black Hand kidnappers Basilo de Stefano, Ciro and Sal Foresture, Antonio Mauro, Giuseppe Granato and Dom Canale (1908), and Gianni Algoni (1911).

"Death Corner," at the intersection of Milton (Cleveland) and Oak, was the subject of many photos because of the number of Black Hand murders that had taken place there. In 1910, a picture was taken of the home of clothing merchant Benedetto Cincnc, who was the victim of an apparent Black Hand murder. In 1911, photos were made of Ignazio D'Amico's bombed-out grocery store at 1050 Milton.

A posed picture of two uniformed Boy Scouts trying to recruit immigrant boys in the Italian district is indicative of the efforts to Americanize young people (1915). Other photos of children in the Italian neighborhoods portray the joy of childhood in the midst of urban poverty. And a photo of women and children dancing at the Chicago Commons settlement house represents the role of such institutions in the development of immigrant communities and individuals.

The *Daily News* collection, by no means complete, captured a number of stereotypical images of Chicago Italians, yet the variety of images provides the modern observer with evidence that there was no one Italian-American experience in Chicago, just as there was no one Little Italy in Chicago. An 1897 *Tribune* article's headlines and subheadings tell quite a story. They read:

> Reigns like King. Mike Rosini and his Odd Monarchy on Dago Flatiron. Unique Italian Colony Members Find Little Annoyance with Poverty and Squalor. Small Shanties Which Are Home to Half a Dozen Families. Persistent Abuse to Charity.

The article's portrayal of an ethnic underclass ruled by a gang and practicing welfare abuse reads like contemporary coverage of black ghetto life in Chicago, except for the "Dago" slur. The article was typical of the many newspaper reports of the era that depicted the hopeless poverty and social problems of Italian immigrants.

It was not uncommon for newspapers to use words to describe ethnic groups that we would today consider outright insults. *L'Italia* conducted a running battle against the use of "Dago." Nevertheless, the Chicago Heights *Star* in 1924 apparently saw nothing wrong with quoting the victim of a robbery as saying that he was accosted by a "gang of Wops." The same paper reported a knife fight between two Calabrians under the headline "Calabrians Carve."

The images and self image that emerge from this sampling are varied: Many Italians lived in slums, many were hardworking, many were socialist, many were gangsters, many were the victims of crimes, many were helped by settlement houses, and many went to church. There were images that made Italians proud and images that shamed them, yet the dynamics of migration depended on the optimism that the success of the next generation would justify the troubles of the present.

Chapter Four

THE ROLE OF THE SCALABRINI FATHERS: A MISSION TO LEAD

Religion and ethnicity are bound together inextricably. They may indeed be the same thing. In Chicago, even in the face of active Americanization programs, the Greeks, the Jews, the Poles, the Irish, the Ukrainians, African Americans, and all the others have used their churches to pass on the language and values of their cultures. The retention of ethnic identity can be greatly enhanced by religious practices and the structures which religious organizations add to the community. The Scalabrini Fathers encouraged the maintenance of Italian language and identity and developed leadership within the community. In every nook and cranny of Italian-American life in Chicago (and in most parts of the country) you are likely to find a Scalabrini priest. Their mission to follow the immigrants and to bring to their communities the Catholic faith has, in fact, evolved into a mission to lead the immigrants. Scalabrinians were behind almost every successful venture in the Italian community. Over the years, they have called the shots and have created an enviable network of institutions and organizations. The history of their work in Chicago is essentially the history of the major Italian American institutions in the Chicago area. But it wasn't always easy.

Early immigrants from Italy were often disaffected from the church. A main theme of Rudolph Vecoli's study of Chicago Italians in the pre–World War I era is the overt anti-clerical attitudes of the mostly unchurched early immigrants. On a personal level, many of the *contadini* had memories of the scandalous behavior by half-educated priests in their southern town in the old country. The Papacy was a major stumbling block to Italian unification. Therefore if you had strong feelings in favor of the unification of Italy and for progress by the Italian government, you had to question the political agenda of the Church. On an economic level, many Italian immigrants believed that ecclesiastic authorities in Rome and in their hometown usually sided with wealthy landlords. The assertive and articulate radical/socialist minority was strongly anti-clerical, spawning the infamous Giordano Bruno Society. Anarchist elements were even more opposed to the Church.

At first, few priests emigrated. The immigrants were on their own. The reception, which faithful Italians received from the Irish and Polish Catholics in Chicago, was a frosty one. Moreover, Italians had such a strong reputation for being "bad Catholics" that Protestant strategists targeted the *paesani* for conversion to the Presbyterian, Lutheran, and Methodist faiths. Italians needed religion. Who would win their hearts and minds? The radicals, the Protestants, or the Catholics?

John Baptist Scalabrini (1839–1905) was born in Lombardy and served as the bishop of Piacenza for a quarter century. Appalled at reports that Italian emigrants were losing contact with the Church, Scalabrini founded a religious congregation of priests and brothers in 1887 in Piacenza. In 1888, seven priests and three lay brothers set out for America and began an odyssey that has engaged the congregation for the last century in an international movement that spans four continents. Some of their mottoes include "bring to the migrant the comfort of the faith and the smile of the homeland" and *Humilitas* (Humility). Their aim is to help immigrants adjust and integrate themselves into the new culture, while maintaining healthy links to their original religion and culture. While their original targets were Italian migrants, when emigration from Italy diminished, they re-focused to minister to a wide variety of migrants. In Chicago and elsewhere, Scalabrini priests have used national and territorial parishes, missions, retreats, radio, television, and newspapers to carry on their mission. Worldwide there are today about 500 Scalabrini priests.

While Bishop Scalabrini can take credit for inspiring a lot of people to work on behalf of the immigrant, his biggest success was the role he played in convincing Mother Frances Xavier Cabrini to drop her plans to go to China and to work among the Italian immigrants instead. She personally worked with Chicago Italians, building a hospital on the Near West Side and staffing the Assumption School with her Sisters of the Sacred Heart. She became the first U.S. citizen to be canonized a saint. Bishop Scalabrini directed his missionaries in the United States and Brazil with encouragement and prudent advice, also sending them financial aid.

Gradually, the Italians and the priests serving them built their own church institutions and these institutions became centers that expressed Italian identity in the Chicago area. Though the Scalabrini Fathers were eventually to dominate, the Servites were the first to establish an Italian parish in Chicago. Assumption Church (1881) was built just north of the river in the shadow of what is now the Merchandise Mart. Assumption School had 500 students by the turn of the century. A second important parish founded by the Servites, St. Philip Benizi (1904–1960s), served large numbers of mostly Sicilian immigrants at a location about a half mile north of Assumption.

In 1903, the Scalabrini Fathers began coming to Chicago. The Province of St. John the Baptist (Midwestern and Western part of the country) grew to include almost a dozen parishes, which the order either founded or took over in the Chicago area. These included Holy Guardian Angel (Near West Side, 1903), Santa Maria Addolorata (Near Northwest Side, 1903), Santa Maria Incoronata (Chinatown, 1904), St. Collistus (Near West Side, 1919), Our Lady of Pompeii (Near West Side, 1910), St. Francis Cabrini (West Side, 1939), St. Anthony of Padua (Roseland, 1904), St. Michael the Archangel (24th and Oakley, 1903), Our Lady of Mount Carmel (Melrose Park, 1905), and St. Charles Boromeo (Stone Park, 1943). Since 1903, dozens of Scalabrini priests nurtured these parishes, their schools, sodalities, and charitable groups. Their letters back home attest to the enormous difficulties of their tasks.

In common with most religious leaders, the Scalabrini Fathers had an "edifice complex." Since all the Italian parishes were new, their leadership focused on continuous campaigns to build and improve additional facilities. Parish histories read like a monotonous litany of what priest came when, what facility he built, how his successor then built an addition, and so on. This litany obscures the fact that there was an enormous struggle going on. In Italy, churches were supported by landholding and endowments accumulated over the centuries, making it unnecessary for individuals to contribute heavily to the Church each Sunday.

Italian immigrant families in Chicago were often living on the edge of poverty and certainly could not afford to lend the kind of financial support that was the custom among the Irish. Many Italian men were not very religious and a good number of them were outright hostile toward the priests whom they regarded as parasites. They resented paying even the nominal parochial school tuition of the era.

Not surprisingly, the rate of Italian children attending parochial school lagged far behind that of the Germans and Polish in Chicago. A 1910 report indicated that only 800 Italian children attended Catholic schools while 20,000 Polish children attended Catholic schools where the language of instruction was Polish. The Chicago Archbishop repeatedly chided the pastors of the Italian churches for not building parish schools at a faster rate. Though a number of new Scalabrini schools were opened between 1910 and 1920,

Italian adherence to the parochial school system continued to lag behind other Catholic Europeans.

The immigrants were *contadini*, mostly illiterate, from the south of Italy, who spoke strange dialects. They were exhausted by their ten-hour work days and their primary loyalties were to their families and their *paesani*. The culture clash between them and the well-educated Scalabrini priests from Northern Italy was considerable. The heroic effort by the Scalabrinians to make good Catholics out of the *paesani* was a difficult one. In contrast to Italy, the freedom and distractions in American society did not automatically give the church or the priest the respect and loyalty that was the norm in Italy. Volunteer associations like the Holy Name Society, the sodalities, school guilds, Christian mothers, fundraising, and other charitable groups had to be built up from square one.

Dealing with their difficult and often changing congregations, while at the same time trying to make personal adjustments to the American church hierarchy and American society, placed the early Scalabrini priests under considerable stress. Their letters back home attest to the enormous difficulties of their tasks. Father Armando Pierini wrote in 1934:

> "In general, I am most disgusted; I feel that I accomplish nothing. There is so much to be done and I succeed at nothing. I sometimes think seriously of going and running away to the top of a mountain far away from everything and everybody. To do good it's true that here in America there are infinite dangers, many more than in Italy" (author's translation).

That was 1934; eventually Father Pierini learned how to fit in quite well.

The relationship between the Chicago Archbishops and the Scalabrinians seems to have been a smooth one and the Chancery office rather willingly left the spiritual care of the Italian population to them. Scalabrinians learned fast and built and rebuilt churches, schools, convents, and rectories and in the process created the social networks necessary for fund raising and community building. Humbert Nelli stresses the role of voluntary associations in the social mobility of Chicago Italians during the 1920s. It was Scalabrini parish activities that fostered and nourished many of those associations.

The Scalabrini movement had some serious competition from non-Catholic religious groups. Pasquale Ricciardi De Carlo was born in Calitri (Avelino) in 1863 of educated parents. At the age of 25 (1888) he came to the United States to establish himself in business and, according to a 1938 commemorative booklet, he met a converted priest who before being called to Chicago in 1914:

> . . . gave him a Bible and urged him to read it. Reportedly, the 3rd and 4th chapters of John gripped him to such an extent that he converted. So anxious was he to spread the Gospel of Jesus Christ that he spent a large portion of his time and money in establishing and helping to organize missions in Providence, RI, Springfield, MA, Hartford, New Haven, Waterbury, and Stanford, CT and Detroit.

De Carlo and his followers believed that:

> . . . the Presbyterian Church with its liberal, social, and educational program . . . offered the greatest promise of successful conservation of the Italian culture in Chicago. It has been the Protestant institution, with its practical, rather than ritualistic, ministry that is playing the leading role in the Christian Americanization process so vital to the welfare of city and nation.

De Carlo came into the "Bloody 19th Ward" on the Near West Side and for a quarter century led the St. John Presbyterian Institutional Church at Harrison and Hoyne. He also directed the Garibaldi Institute, "a Neighborhood House" at 904 S. Oakley.

De Carlo's early years were tough. He had to overcome indifference and superstition of Italian settlers and the prejudice and antagonism toward Protestantism that had been instilled in them by the Catholic Church. His response was to organize Americanization classes, kindergartens, mothers' clubs, prayer meetings, Boy Scout troops, a Bureau of Information and Employment, and other activities.

Reverend De Carlo was very successful at raising funds from wealthy non-Italian Presbyterians. He got George H. Jones, for instance, to give $175,000 for the construction of the Garibaldi Institute. Samuel Insull was on his donors' list. While the St. John's Board consisted entirely of Italian-named males, only two of the 100 male and female names on the donors' list were Italian. He reportedly played an important role in getting Jones, of Inland Steel in Chicago Heights, to donate a large sum to construct the Harold Colbert Jones Community Center, which served many Italians in that city.

Over the years, De Carlo produced Italian language publications like *Il Cittadino*, *La Fiamma*, and *Vita Nuova* (later *Il Progresso di Chicago*). His emphasis on patriotism, both Italian and American, was meant to appeal to Italians who were disaffected from the Catholic Church, which had traditionally opposed Italian national unity. His ability to provide social services and employment through his connections with established Presbyterians in the city was another important element in his success.

In 1938, a St. John's fundraising brochure claimed attendance at all its events and programs for the year at 58,000. That included 36,000 in educational and vocational groups that, in turn, included 17,000 in the 14–20 age group and almost 10,000 in the 9–13 group. St. John extended "Relief Work" to 1,300 families.

Protestantism also played an important role in the Chicago Heights Italian community. In 1910, the First Presbyterian Church appointed Reverend Eugenio De Luca to make a pitch for support within the Italian community by founding the Church of Our Savior (eventually located at 24th and Wallace in the Hill neighborhood). Under the leadership of Reverend De Luca, the Bible-oriented church used a combination of social services, social functions, and help in finding jobs to pull together a close-knit group of up to 200 Protestant Italian Americans who participated in a dizzying whirl of Bible readings, choir practices, drama performances, youth activities, picnics, parties, and sporting events.

Whether these activities were a cause or effect, Protestant Italians in Chicago Heights seemed to Americanize at a faster rate and to move into business positions and the professions at a slightly faster rate than did Catholic Italians. A possible explanation for this may be that this church, like the early Puritans, stressed English literacy so that its members could read the Bible. This opportunity to increase their English fluency and their exposure to American culture afforded by church activities speeded up the assimilation process.

Although it was accorded a good deal of favorable publicity by *The Star*, the Church of Our Savior never represented more than seven percent of the Italians in the Chicago Heights. Harsh feelings and name-calling between Catholics and Protestants seemed to characterize the relationship between the two in the early days. Old-timers remember an incident in the early 1920s in which Catholic rowdies led "Svoboda's blind horse" into the sacristy of the little Protestant church. In 1915, Reverend De Luca was also among the group that organized the aforementioned Jones Community Center on the East Side of Chicago Heights.

Giuseppe Maria Abbate was a Neapolitan barber who was remanded to the Elgin State Hospital for the criminally insane in the 1930s, accused of statutory rape. In a bizarre chapter of Chicago history, this man attracted hundreds of Italians on the West Side to his pseudo-Catholic cult from 1919 to the early 1930s. Abbate dressed like the Pope. He claimed to have experienced a vision and to have been called by God to be his *Messegero Celeste* (Celestial Messenger).

His basic "theological" teaching was that he and his followers were the reincarnation of the Virgin Mary and the saints. Photos in a rather slick magazine published by the cult in 1927 show him with a sword, cape, and helmet, protecting a child identified as "the Madonna Child Reincarnated at one year of age in the arms of the Celestial Messenger, her spiritual protector." With his barber chair in the left foreground and a child identified as "the Virgin Mary at age 12" in the right foreground, Padre Celeste decked himself out in full regalia (including a Papal scull cap) and sat at his desk for yet another bizarre photo. (See the author's *Images of America: Italians in Chicago* for this photo).

The cult's headquarters (reportedly at 548 W. DeKoven Street) was an old home decked out with banners and flags extolling "*Il Messeggero Celeste*." Inside, the parlor (*Il Sacro Tempio*) was crammed with a Catholic-style altar, opulent chandeliers, candles, draperies, and flowers. A charismatic figure, Abbate performed one known miracle: He was able to get his Italian followers to tithe themselves! For obvious financial and other reasons, his cult was not large or long-lived. Few today have a living memory of this Celestial phenomenon. Those who seek further information should consult the Italian American Collection at the University of Illinois at Chicago.

After establishing the parishes and schools, the next logical step was the creation of a seminary. Provincial Beniamino Franch was anxious to fulfill the dream of having a Scalabrini Seminary in the United States. It would act like a perpetual motion machine: from the children of the immigrants would come the priests to minister to the immigrants.

The point man on this project was the youthful Father Armando Pierini, who was destined to become the most accomplished leader in the history of Chicago's Italians. Born in Agello, Province of Perugia, in 1908, Pierini was ordained in 1932 in Piacenza. After a short sojourn as rector for students at the Gregorian University in Rome, Pierini was assigned as assistant to Father Joseph Bernardi at the Santa Maria Addolorata Church. Influenced by the presence of Our Lady of Mount Carmel in Melrose Park, Franch and Pierini chose nearby Stone Park as the site for the new Sacred Heart Seminary.

The dedication ceremony for the new building in May 1937 drew a crowd of 10,000. In attendance were the cardinal, apostolic delegates, and reporters and photographers from the metropolitan press.

Beginning with a class of ten, the fledgling seminary took students from age 14 and stressed liberal arts, philosophy, and the Italian language in its high school- and college-level curriculum. A half dozen priests and a few lay teachers served the residential student body. Enrollment never got much beyond 60. As Pierini explained it:

> I was chosen to be rector and I remained rector of the seminary for 11 years. It was completed in May 1937. We had lay teachers, I taught a lot of the subjects myself without knowing a lot about them, but that's the way it goes. The students lived right there. The third floor was the dormitory, the second floor was classrooms and the first floor was office and chapel. We started with about 10 and then it went up to 40 or 50.

Yet, before it was phased out in the mid 1960s, the Sacred Heart Seminary had trained perhaps 100 Italian-American men for the priesthood and for leadership in the Chicago Italian community and beyond. Moreover, the seminary trained a number of men who did not ultimately become priests, but who as laymen played important leadership roles in Italian-American organizations in the city.

During the early post–World War II era, the Sacred Heart Seminary had become, without question, the focal center for the Scalabrini movement—the natural place for solving the citywide problems of Italian Americans. Though the parishes now had churches, schools, and convents, they were not equipped to deal with a new demographic reality for Italians in Chicago: a sizable cohort of the immigrants who had been healthy enough to reach old age and whose family members were not always able to take care of them. New concerns about the elderly within the Italian-American community had to be met with a citywide organization.

One of the first to perceive the change and to plan for it was Father Pierini. On October 12, 1945, he scheduled a gathering at the seminary for what was ostensibly just another Columbus Day banquet. But it was more. Father Pierini had yet another ambitious project to propose to the lay and clerical representatives from the dozen Scalabrini parishes—an Italian Old People's Home. A strong contingent of those present, led by church loyalist Joseph De

Serto (who was later to become Pierini's closest ally and confidante), argued in favor of a citywide Scalabrinian Catholic high school for Italian American boys. Pierini's idea won out.

The first order of business was to seek an audience with the cardinal, which was granted in December of 1945. Speaking in Italian, Cardinal Stritch reluctantly granted approval for the project, attaching to his approval a series of substantial reservations. He refused to allow title to the prospective institution to be held by the Fathers of St. Charles, even though other orders had been allowed that privilege before and since. He also stipulated that no hard planning should proceed until the Italian community had collected $300,000 in funds up front.

Committee members came away with mixed feelings. While they got provisional approval, it was almost as if the cardinal didn't expect the plan to materialize. And it was perhaps this skepticism that challenged and motivated the committee to achieve their goals. It was in this period that Father Pierini's team began to form: Joseph De Serto, an insurance man with a penchant for organization; John Congelosi, an artist; Judge Louis Senese, a Melrose Park magistrate; and Marco De Stefano, an insurance agent with good contacts at the chancery and the Knights of Columbus.

The Scalabrini Fathers broke ground for the new retirement home in 1949. In 1951, they opened the doors to the old people's home, christened "Villa Scalabrini." After that 1945 meeting there followed 45 years of endless carnivals, banquets, stage shows, bingos, raffles, and every other imaginable method of fund raising. The Villa Scalabrini grew to become a proud $20 million institution serving 250 residents. The process of striving to achieve this goal has in itself created a community of interest among Italians that has replaced the neighborhood-based geographic communities of the pre–World War II era. Until the Villa slipped out of the control of the Scalabrini Fathers in the 1990s, it stood as a citadel protecting, preserving, and inventing Italian-American culture and identity.

None of original backers of the Villa were wealthy. The *prominenti* were eventually to jump on the Villa bandwagon in various stages. The fact that they were not the most wealthy and prominent sometimes led them and others to doubt that they could pull off the ambitious task they had set for themselves. At the beginning the qualities that these men seemed to share were an unusual (for Italian men) devotion to the Catholic faith and strong personal attachments to the Scalabrini priests in their parishes. In 1946 Pierini started his own radio show, "L'Ora Cattolica" on which he prophesied during an August broadcast:

> I envision, rising in the country, amid green fields and in the shade of trees, a large and beautiful edifice. There in peace and in the midst of flowers our oldsters stroll, with a smile, with their faces expressing a profound satisfaction. They will have Italian sisters to take care of them like little mothers; they will have a beautiful chapel where they may bare their souls in prayer; they will have facilities where they may pass their days at their preferred hobbies or pastime. There will be a gay dining room; a clean and well equipped infirmary; above all each of our aged will have his own little room, all his own with every comfort. This dream must become a reality because it is an act of charity desired by God but it will become a tangible reality only if every Italian family, every individual of our community takes this cause to heart and assumes his part of the responsibility. It will take a half million dollars to have a home adequate to meet the need of the entire community; let us not become frightened, a half million is not so great a sum when you consider that there are 400,000 Italians in the Chicago area.
>
> Pierini's weekly efforts yielded a steady stream of contributions from his listeners and the commercial Italian broadcasters soon joined in the effort to reach that non-geographical Italian community.

The committee also planned a door-to-door campaign in the Italian neighborhoods and they enlisted the commercial Italian language broadcasters Stefano Luotto, Serena Notari, Nicola Francone, Americo Lupi, Amabile Santa Caterina, and Antonio Faustini to publicize the campaign and encourage listeners to welcome the solicitors from the Italian Old People's Home. The radio campaign softened prospective donors and it generated mail responses.

Not long afterward, Pierini received a crumpled envelope addressed in shaky Italian handwriting. It contained 22 $500 gold certificates with an anonymous note specifying that $500 be used for the radio program, $500 go to masses (for the donor's special intention), and $10,000 be used for the proposed home for the Italian Aging. The magic of this anonymous donation energized Pierini and his associates.

Although each success was a new adventure, the founders were still a long way from their ultimate goal and doubt still remained as to whether they could achieve it. But when, against all odds, the committee was able to sell 1,000 $25 tickets to a banquet in 1947, they knew that they were on their way.

Another major means of reaching the Italian-American public in Chicago during the late 1940s and the 1950s was through the parishes. In 1947, Father Luigi Donanzan of St. Michael's Church developed a formula for involving the parishes in a citywide Italian festival that supported the Villa project. The post-war period was a different world from the one we know—a simpler one. The pleasure of carnival rides and games and the prospect of winning a new Studebaker or television or vacuum cleaner were almost irresistible to the average working family of that era. When organizers added to those incentives radio and stage celebrities, the exhibition of an iron lung (then used to treat victims of TB), a popularity contest, and Italian food, they created a money machine. For the next ten years the Italian festival became a main source of fund raising for the old people's home.

Originated by Donanzan, based on his experience in Kansas City, then perfected to a science by Joe De Serto, the festival was a three-week affair held first at Roosevelt Road and Cicero, then at other near west suburban locations. Pierini enlisted the support of an army of 500 volunteers for the length of the run. Each parish had its own concession and each contributed volunteers to the general cause. Logistics of the operation are impressive: planning began in January, drainage ditches had to be dug in case of rain, concessionaires, carnival rides, liquor permits, security arrangements, political cooperation, poster advertising, bad weather insurance, transportation for volunteers, arrangements for electricians, donations of prizes, booking of entertainers—all had to be planned and organized. The 1948 flyer invites the public to partake of 500 barrels of beer, 5 tons of sausage and beef, 20,000 $1 spaghetti dinners. All this, and a tilt-a-whirl, too, brought in a phenomenal $99,000 the first year and a decreasing but respectable amount in subsequent years. As Pierini confirmed:

> The idea of a big carnival, festivals, was Father Louis Donazan's who had experience with festivals in Kansas City, MO. It went over in an unthinkable way, it was fantastic! We had maybe over $100,000 and big bands and people, we had over 500 people that came every single night from the Scalabrini Churches . . . to serve, to cook, to help out. The Italian people wanted an old people's home for their old folks!

In addition to the fund raising, the festivals created a sense of involvement and community among people from all the Scalabrini parishes, and they created a sense of identity with and a feeling of ownership of the emerging old people's home among the thousands of volunteers over the years. In fact, Father Lawrence Cozzi (who succeeded Pierini as director of the Villa Scalabrini) first became aware of the old people's home when he worked as a boy volunteer for the St. Callistus jar game.

In the late 1950s, the carnivals and the Villa project began to lose some support from beleaguered pastors in the dwindling neighborhoods. As worthy a project as the Villa Scalabrini was, it was drawing more than its share of the charity and attention of the community. Proud pastors resented being referred to as "Villa Scalabrini priests." This problem challenged Father Pierini to find yet another means of reaching the Italian Americans in the Chicago area.

As the original immigrant generation died off, Italian language broadcasting was becoming less effective. An English-language medium was needed to reach the second and third generation families who were dispersing from the old neighborhoods into scattered suburbs. An English-language Italian-American newspaper was the answer. One wonders why ethnic leaders had not thought of it earlier. In April 1960, Pierini won approval from the lay Scalabrini League to support the launching of *Fra Noi.*

A modest newsletter during its first few months, the paper proclaimed its desire "to bring us together once a month and thus rekindle in our midst the spirit of cooperation and union which should be ours through common heritage." As he had in earlier campaigns, Father Pierini and a corps of volunteers combed the metropolitan phone books to produce a list of 40,000 Italian names to whom the newspaper was sent gratis for the first year. The nominal annual subscription price was $1.

For most of its history, Father Pierini served as editor, with the assistance of Mary Mugnanini and Lola Pocci. In the late 1960s and early 1970s, Father Paul Asciolla, a young social activist, edited *Fra Noi* and in the late 1970s, Father Lawrence Cozzi worked on the paper. Melrose Park photographer Sam Bruno acted as Pierini's side-kick at community events and took thousands of photos that appeared in the paper. An amazing number of them showed Father Pierini with a smile on his face accepting a check from a proud donor to one of the Villa's latest projects. Before the 1980s, the paper never had any paid professional reporters—relying instead on contributed columns, news releases, reports written by club officials, and a few stories written by the editor. Emil Stubits, and later Jack Kuenster, were professional printers and were paid a stipend to turn the editorial copy into the finished newspaper.

The 500 monthly issues published regularly since 1960 are a rich chronicle of Italian Americana. In the early years, *Fra Noi* was strictly a public relations instrument, a house organ for Villa Scalabrini. Positive information about the growth and development of the Villa was highlighted. The core of the publication consisted of upcoming fund-raising events that rated full-page ads, stories, and pictures. Reminders to remember the Villa in your will were woven in with touching photos of the Villa residents in a campaign called "Villa Scalabrini is . . . "

Though not a big money maker, the venture usually broke even through the sale of advertising to Italian funeral homes, Alitalia, caterers, banks, and Italian-American businessmen friendly to the cause. Through *Fra Noi*, the Villa acted as a social arbiter, conferring prestige on its benefactor in stories and especially with pictures of their activities. Another regular feature was the honor roll of donors listing with the amounts they had pledged. While this is pretty much standard fare for a house organ, there was more.

Fra Noi fulfilled a cultural and political mission for Chicago's Italians as it became a city-wide communications medium, replacing the informal neighborhood networks of earlier years. The *Fra Noi* held up a mirror to the Italian-American community to show what it was, to suggest where it should be going, and to encourage Italian Americans to keep identifying with their own. Cleverly, *Fra Noi* was mirroring a sense of community even while it was helping to create a new sense of a new community. Recognition of the work of ethnic activists and contributions in *Fra Noi* encouraged and expanded those good works, promoting their retention and preserving a sense of community purpose, beyond the natural inclinations of the community. In short, the mere illusion that a healthy Italian-American community existed helped to create a healthy Italian-American community.

According to the image presented in the paper, the community joyously celebrated Columbus Day, bitterly resented all Mafia smears in the media, and piously practiced Catholicism. Over the years, the newspaper collected a series of columnists whose diversity, talents, and folksiness reflected the community. Maurice Marchello, a Roseland lawyer in the early 1960s, contributed a dozen articles on *paesani* groups, their home towns in Italy, and their accomplishments in Chicago. He eventually published two nostalgic books of essays, *Crossing the Tracks* and *Black Coal, White Bread*, largely based upon the columns that he originally did for *Fra Noi*.

Guy Lanzilotti, on the editorial staff of the *Chicago Sun-Times* for many years, wrote a monthly column on contemporary political issues facing Italian Americans, such as the Immigration Reform Bill, the possibility of Italy going communist, and the effectiveness of Ohio Governor Michael DiSalle. From the very beginning, until 1975, Stefano Luotto edited an Italian language page (*pagina in Italiano*) that focused on news from Italy. After 1975 the Italian page was edited by Father Pierini, a minimal concession to Italian-language constituents.

It was through his columns in *Fra Noi* that Victor Arrigo first came to prominence among Chicago Italians. His chauvinistic but well-informed pieces on Italian heroes like Verdi, Brumidi, Tonti, and Judge Musmanno led him to teach a course entitled "Sojourn in Italy" in 1963, which was attended by some 500 Italian Americans thirsty for self-knowledge. In 1966, Arrigo was elected to the Illinois State Legislature where he gained recognition for adding an ethnic anti-defamation clause to the 1970 Illinois Constitution. It read:

> Individual Dignity. To promote individual dignity, communications that portray criminality, depravity or lack of virtue in, or that incite violence, hatred, abuse or hostility toward, a person or group of persons by reason of or by reference to religious, racial, ethnic, national or regional affiliation are condemned.

That provision in the Illinois Constitution was used (unsuccessfully) by the American Italian Defense Association as the basis for a lawsuit against the producers of the *Sopranos* TV show. The consensus is that Arrigo owed his political career to *Fra Noi*.

Fra Noi covered sports—stories about high school athletes sharing space with articles about Ron Santo, Joe Pepitone, and Rocky Marciano in the early 1960s. Popular WLS disc jockey Dick Biondi contributed a short-lived series targeting Italian-American teens. *Fra Noi* also covered the Chicago visit of Il Re di Maggio—former Italian King Umberto.

Social commentary from Anthony Sorrentino, a sociologist who was among the leaders in the Illinois Commission for Delinquency Prevention, began in March 1964 with a column on the growing importance of the Joint Civic Committee of Italian Americans (JCCIA) under the patronage of Congressman Frank Annunzio. By the 1960s, the leadership in the Joint Civic Committee had forged a strong alliance with Villa Scalabrini, Father Pierini, and *Fra Noi*. It might even be said that *Fra Noi* became a house organ for the JCCIA. As ever, anti-defamation (against Mafia stereotyping) was a surefire way to create close links between Italian Americans.

Annunzio and Arrigo are only the most striking examples of *Fra Noi*'s political efforts. Observers like to point out that before 1960, Italian-American politicians in the Chicago area were few and far between. Today there are dozens of elected officials on all levels of government in the state. While it might be difficult to prove a direct causal relationship, around election time *Fra Noi* blossomed with paid display advertising for Italian candidates from both parties. News stories extolled their virtues. Few Italian-American politicians would omit *Fra Noi* from their campaign plans. Even non-Italian candidates used *Fra Noi* as a medium to reach its targeted readership. Ironically, in 1984 this Catholic Italian paper that had previously promoted the candidacy of everyone with an Italian name found itself at odds with itself over the Geraldine Ferraro's 1984 Vice Presidential candidacy on the abortion issue.

Fra Noi was sometimes able to mobilize support for causes as well as candidates. Lyndon Johnson's 1965 Immigration Reform Bill didn't just happen. It was the result of political pressure from groups like The American Committee on Italian Migration (ACIM). For three consecutive issues, *Fra Noi* beseeched its readers to join the December 14, 1963 ACIM rally at McCormick Place on behalf of the new immigration bill. The pleas netted a respectable crowd of 5,000 on that bitter cold December day. The featured speaker was Senator Paul Douglas. Until the 1980s, *Fra Noi* was under the direct editorship of Father Pierini except for a period in the late 1960s to 1976 when Father Paul Asciolla co-directed the paper. If Pierini was a forthright ethnic advocate, the much younger Asciolla was a militant in the age of White Ethnicity. Linked to inter-ethnic organizations such as the American Jewish Committee's Illinois Consultation on Ethnicity in Education and Monsignor Geno Baroni's National Center for Urban Ethnic Affairs, Asciolla sharpened the focus of the paper. Under his tutelage, *Fra Noi* ran questionnaires on the new white ethnicity, excerpts from Greeley's *Why Can't They be Like Us*, book reviews of serious works published by the American Italian Historical Association, 12 notices of AIHA conferences, and even Rudolph Vecoli's famous autobiographical essay, "Color me Red, White, and Green." *Fra Noi* also campaigned for a national Italian-American organization.

Under Asciolla the paper was more dramatic in both content and in format in its political support of Italian candidates, (notably Annunzio in his crucial 1972 election). Asciolla had alliances with the metropolitan media—appearing on early morning television and late night radio at a dizzying pace. He was also the subject of a well-publicized interview on white ethnicity by Bill Moyers. Despite his endorsement of George McGovern in the 1972 election and Jimmy Carter in 1976, Asciolla and *Fra Noi* maintained the support of the Italian-American community, until Asciolla's departure to join Geno Baroni's National Center on

Urban Ethnicity and the National Italian American Foundation in Washington in the summer of 1976.

In 1984, Father Pierini at 76 continued to edit *Fra Noi.* The perennial group photos and check presentations were as much a fixture in the 1984 issues as they were in 1964. The honor roll of donors remained. There was still no paid editorial staff. Though most of the early columnists were gone, Tony Sorrentino continued to contribute two or three big stories on events, people, and ideas each month. Ann Sorrentino's exquisite food column remained a staple and her columns were collected in an outstanding cookbook *From Ann's Kitchen.* Annunzio did a regular column from Washington. Mario Avignone's "Petals from Roseland" column offered updates and news of (former) residents. A new effort seemed to be underway to publicize internal activities at the Villa. Italian-American businessmen and politicians continued advertising. The circulation has stabilized at about 10,000.

In March of 1985, *Fra Noi* changed. Pierini retired as editor and was replaced by former *Sun-Times* journalist Jim Ylisela. In the first month of Ylisela's editorship the appearance of the paper changed radically. The masthead *Fra Noi* was enlarged and a touch of red and green ran on the front page. Almost immediately the number of pages increased to 32, advertising increased by almost 100 percent, and the photos showed a new perspective. Ylisela brought in with him a team of young writers, including Fred Gardaphé (who became editor of the cultural section) and Pamela DiFiglio, whose first big assignment was a pull-out section on Italian-American women. Professional journalists Paul Basile and Phil Franchine also began doing regular feature stories on such topics as the Taylor Street and Harlem Avenue neighborhoods. An editorial section and letters to the editor feature were added.

Father Pierini's role in the paper was relegated to editing a two-page Italian language section. Sorrentino's monthly contribution was limited to his popular "People in the News" column and Joint Civic Committee activities were bumped off their perennial front page placement. Avignone's "Petals from Roseland" continued to bloom as did Congressman Annunzio's report from Washington and Ann Sorrentino's food column. Other parts of the paper were organized by departments.

Some questioned whether a professional journalist who was not a community insider could or should handle the job of editor. Minor snafus in paste-up, which misidentified well-known Villa supporters, seemed to confirm their negative judgment. On the other hand, many welcomed the expansion of *Fra*

Noi to include Italian-American people who were not previously identified with the Villa. At last, they hoped, *Fra Noi* had made the transformation from an organ of the Villa to become a paper "Serving Chicagoland's Italian American Communities," as the masthead proclaimed. They welcomed the new focus on a wider range of people and institutions that made up the Italian-American community in Chicago.

As publisher of the paper, Father Cozzi made a commitment to the staff that allowed for professionalization of the publication. Some editors and reporters were now paid small stipends for their services and the reading public no longer had to depend upon news releases submitted (or not submitted) by publicity chairpersons of the various Italian organizations.

Five years later Paul Basile took over as editor and after a stormy transition period, ownership of the *Fra Noi* was totally transferred from the Scalabrini Order to a board of directors headed up by Anthony Fornelli, an attorney who was the former president of Unico and who had been the driving force behind Chicago's Festa Italiana. Under Basile's aggressive leadership the *Fra Noi* grew larger—55 pages of news, columns, and features in English, nine pages in Italian, a score of "special advertising" pages devoted to the news of the various clubs, and lots of advertising—for a total of 136 pages. Many of the columns were also offered as national features to other Italian-American newspapers across the country. Father Pierini's modest four page newsletter has indeed come a long way. Twenty-first century Chicago Italian Americans had found an effective voice.

Fra Noi became the most important ancillary activity supporting the Villa. Together, the paper and the home for the elderly formed a focal center for the Chicago Italian-American community. Indeed, it would be hard to conceive of any meaningful way the term "community" could be used to describe Chicago's Italians if the *Fra Noi* and the Villa Scalabrini did not exist.

A very effective strategy developed by Father Pierini in the 1960s was to "infiltrate" every Italian-American organization, the ethnic clubs, in the city. The goal was to tie all the groups to the Villa and to encourage them to compete with one another in their charity toward the Villa. The strategy worked. It strengthened the Villa and it strengthened the clubs.

For 20 years the St. Charles Seminary functioned very well. Then changing religious attitudes led to decreased vocations in the 1960s and the Scalabrini Order consolidated locations for its seminaries. The building fell into disuse. But, like the phoenix, the seminary rose again, as the Italian Cultural Center in the 1970s. The newer buildings was converted into the Casa Italia in the late 1990s.

The Italian Cultural Center was established in the original seminary in the early 1970s by Father August Feccia. In his spiritual work, Feccia had been shocked to learn that Chicago's Italians had little functional awareness of the Italian language or the cultural heritage of Italy. With the cooperation of John Bucci, John Cadel, Leonora LiPuma, Colonel Frank Chesrow, and many others, Feccia organized a series of ambitious art and cultural programs to coincide with the country's bicentennial celebration in 1976. He personally did some of the reconstruction work to adapt the building; he ran the printing press to publish Joseph Tusiani's book of poetry (*Gente Mia*), and he personally begged and bought the works of original art for the center's Cadel Gallery.

The center also sponsored a choral and dance group led by Josephine LiPuma, which performed at over 100 functions per year. A professional librarian, Florence Roselli, volunteered to organize a library for the center and the building eventually was also equipped with classrooms for music and Italian language instruction to adults and children, a radio recording studio, the Italians in Chicago historical photo exhibit, a (1 to 100 ratio) miniature of St. Peter's Square, an exhibit on Bishop Scalabrini, and rooms dedicated to World War II veterans, and one dedicated to the Calabresi in America. In addition, the center offers immigrant pension counseling service.

Father Gino Dalpiaz (himself a product of the Sacred Heart Seminary) leads a program that blends the religious and the artistic with an emphasis on Italian language radio broadcasting and youth. Recent funding from Italy and from the state of Illinois has helped the center to expand language instruction. Though sometimes in competition with the Italian government's *Istituto Italiano di Cultura* for leadership in cultural programming, the center is unrivaled as the cultural institution most closely serving Italian Americans. As part of the Casa Italia complex, it has become the cultural home of the Italian-American community.

In recent decades there has been some slippage in the amount of influence that the Scalabrini priests have in Italian parishes in Chicago. In part this is due to the fact that Italian Americans have moved out of the inner city ethnic parishes and scattered in the suburbs. The Order gave up Santa Maria Incoronata in the mid-1980s and that church became a Chinese mission. Santa Maria Addolorata, on the near northwest side, though still run by Scalabrini priests, is heavily Hispanic. And St. Anthony of Padua in the Roseland area is also Hispanic, with a small contingent of Italian Americans who come in from the suburbs for Sunday mass. Our Lady of Pompeii Church has become an independent shrine. And, of course, the Holy Guardian Angel Church and school were victims of urban renewal in the 1960s.

In the 1990s, even the Villa Scalabrini slipped from the control of the Order. In contrast to Father Pierini's personal management of a place for Italian old people in the 1950s, the management of health care facilities in the 1990s had become a big business involving the bureaucracies of state and federal welfare systems, licensing, and the politics of the archdiocese. Since the Archbishop of Chicago had always held the title to the property, final decisions on the fate of the facility proved to be beyond the scope of the Italian community, which had worked so hard for 40 years to raise the money to build and expand the institution of which they were so proud. Management of Villa Scalabrini passed over to the Redemptorist Fathers. While the loss of the Villa was a severe blow to the community, the change in administration could not erase the bonds of community that had been created in the process of building the institution. The Villa was the cause that brought about the *Fra Noi* and it was the cause that gave the Joint Civic Committee and the other clubs a noble goal to strive for and a reason to show unity with other Italian Americans.

In spite of these reversals, the Scalabrini Fathers are more influential among Chicago Italians than in any other city in the United States. It is doubtful if any other group, religious or otherwise, has had as much influence in shaping the Italian ethnicity in the United States as has the Scalabrini Order.

When compared with the resources and manpower of the Scalabrinians, lay Italian-American institutions in Chicago and throughout the nation seem weak and scattered. Nor do they have the link with Italian culture that the mostly Italian-speaking Scalabrinians have. The regional associations, service organizations, and social clubs have been co-opted into relationships with the Villa, the Cultural Center, and other Scalabrinian ventures. Their contributions finance the initiative and leadership of the Scalabrinians. The historic challengers to the Scalabrinians are no more. Anti-clerical socialists are gone; the Italian Protestants are few and far between; and the renegade Catholic movement of Padre Celeste is only a dim quaint memory.

In Chicago, the Scalabrini priests are no longer called upon to minister to the poor and illiterate Italian Americans; the people whom they serve are no longer needy in a material sense. As an Order, the Scalabrinians have widened their scope of interest beyond Italian immigrants to embrace all immigrants: Mexicans to California; Filipinos to Canada; South Americans to Florida. This change will, no doubt, have an impact on the style and substance of the role that Scalabrinians will play among Chicago's Italians in coming years.

The Scalabrinians built their temple well and have outlasted all rivals, lay and religious. Though the Sacred Heart Seminary and the Villa Scalabrini were not long term successes, they served their purposes. They had a good run.

And while observers might quibble about the lack of democratic participation in the personnel and policy decisions of the Order and about the wisdom of placing so much leadership responsibility in the hands of foreign born priests sent here from Piacenza and Rome, the Scalabrini Fathers of St. Charles have aroused very little opposition. Most would agree that the Order saved the faith of the Italians in Chicago, while providing them with major institutions for nourishing and maintaining the Italian language, culture, identity, and a sense of community.

Chapter Five

THE POWER GAME: ITALIANS IN CHICAGO POLITICS

"Politics ain't Bean Bag" is an old saying in Chicago. That sentiment can be applied across the board to all aspects of big (and small) city society. As Martin Scorcese has illustrated in the film *Gangs of New York* and as Glazier and Moynihan have shown in their break-through *Beyond the Melting Pot* study of New York City ethnic groups, the rough and tumble of urban life is a constant scramble for power and place where rules are often bent. Once Italian immigrants to Chicago progressed past the survival era, they got into the scramble for power in a big way. As individuals, families and groups, they jumped into the fray with gusto. With varying degrees of success, they sought their share (and more) of power in politics, business, and organized labor. In keeping with that part of the American spirit that honors success at any price, they chose licit and, occasionally, illicit enterprises to reach their goals.

Ethnic groups have always placed high importance on electing their own. Officeholders of one's own ethnic group give access and pride and, it is assumed, power. Sometimes these hopes are fulfilled; but over-expectation can be dangerous. There has never been an "Italian Political Agenda" as such and one need only to look to Italy to see the wide range of disagreement on fundamental economic and social issues. In a sense, those who put great stock in electing people with Italian names in expectation of broad benefits for the entire group are programmed for disappointment. And when Italian-American candidates run against each other, the whole concept of ethnic politics becomes muddled.

While the significance of ethnic political power should not be overrated, neither should it be undervalued. Successful politicians provide role models for others in the ethnic group. Every officeholder brings with him or her a retinue of friends and family who derive social and economic benefits that can have a ripple effect throughout the ethnic community.

Into the 1950s, Italians clustered in neighborhoods north, south, and west of the Loop business district. Significant additional Italian colonies sprang up in the suburbs of Melrose Park, Chicago Heights, Blue Island, and Highwood.

Downstate, in such places as Spring Valley, Cherry, and Herrin, Italian coal miners and former coal miners settled. Though ethnic population statistics are always somewhat suspect, it appears that by the 1920s Italians made up about 5 percent of Chicago's population. This figure has remained relatively steady throughout the last decades of the century and in the absence of high profile issues, outstanding leaders, and coalition building, there would seem to be no reason to expect political dominance from Italians in Chicago.

If you don't vote, you don't count. Writing about the political interaction of ethnic groups in Chicago before 1936, John Allswang observed of the Italians that they were relative latecomers to the scene—82 percent of them arriving here after 1900—after the rules had been set and the Irish had ensconced themselves in the police and fire departments. Moreover, apparently practicing the sojourner mentality, Italians were slow to apply for citizenship. Even by 1920, only 35 percent of Italians had obtained citizenship and the right to vote. That is about half the rate of the foreign-born Irish, Swedish, German, and Norwegian population. The lag in female citizenship and voting among Italians was another debilitating factor. On the other hand, political machines sometimes finagled ways to get non-citizens on the voters list anyway. In any case, interest in political participation among all immigrants advanced in the 1920s when Prohibition enforcement became a major local issue.

On the national level, Italian Americans generally supported the Republican party. Whether this was an aversion to Woodrow Wilson's racism and his anti-Italian stance on the Trieste issue in the Versailles Treaty is unclear. Competition with Chicago's Irish, who controlled the local Democratic Party, may also have been a factor in pushing Italians toward the Republican column. *L'Italia* generally supported the Republican Party on the national level. Moreover, Capone's alliance with Republican Mayor William Hale "Big Bill" Thompson gave Italian voters yet another reason to support the GOP. Italian voters seemed to break ranks in 1928 to support Democrat Al Smith, who was the first Catholic major party presidential nominee. Later, Franklin Roosevelt brought Italians and most other ethnic groups into his winning Democratic coalition. Like everyone else in a close election, Italians in Chicago can credibly argue that it was their support of John F. Kennedy that got him elected in Illinois in 1960. Later in the decade, nationwide Italian Americans slipped over into the comfortable Republican middle class.

Since the 1930s, the Democratic Party has been the only game in town in Chicago. Successful Italian political operatives from the city tend to be Democrats

Continued on page 97

Pictured in the Palmo Bar on 1858 W. Huron Street in 1950, from left to right are: John and Stella Folak, Joseph Purpura , Delores, Palmo Abbinante, his daughter Mary Abbinante Purpura (wife of Joe), Wally Folak, "Duke," Joe Blazak, Jim Folak (seated), Jerry, Leonard, and Ronald.

The worshippers at Our Lady of Pompeii Church, Columbus Day Mass in the early 1980s included Fred Mazzei, the Columbus Day Queen and her Court, Ann Sorrentino, Leonard Giampietro, Theresa Petrone, Josephine LiPuma, Mary Cutean, Angela Zaranti, Diane Corradetti, and scores of people active in the Italian-American community.

Scalabrinian Father Armando Pierini was a prime mover in the founding of the Sacred Heart Seminary, the Villa Scalabrini, and the Fra Noi *newspaper. As the most effective leader in the Italian-American community, Pierini's life story illustrates the great impact that his religious order had in preserving the culture and religious faith of Italians in Chicago.*

Father Pierini's idea of an Italian Old People's home proved so successful that it was copied by Scalabrinians in California. The benefactor for Villa Scalabrini-Sun Valley was Frank Sinatra. In this 1983 photo he presents a $50,000 check to the charity. Among those looking on are Congressman Frank Annunzio and Father Lawrence Cozzi.

The Feast of St. Joseph of Bagheria in the 1930s wends its way along Cambridge Avenue toward St. Philip Benizi Church. Note the African-American family seated in the left foreground.

One of the Balbo's seaplanes sits at rest in the harbor north of Navy Pier in 1933. The trans-oceanic flight of Balbo's squadron of 24 planes ignited the pride of Chicago Italians more than any other event in history.

LOGGIA SUPREMA

LIBERTÀ UGUAGLIANZA FRATELLANZA

ORDINE FIGLI D'ITALIA IN AMERICA

Noi Venerabile Supremo e Segretario
Archivista Supremo della Loggia Suprema dell'Ordine Figli d'Italia in America

in virtù del potere investitoci dalle Leggi dell'Ordine, dietro raccomandazione ed approvazione del Gran Concilio Esecutivo dello Stato di Illinois e ratifica del Concilio Esecutivo Supremo, diamo il nostro pieno consenso e la nostra autorità agli amati fratelli

— Alex J. Adducci — Domenic Lupo — Vincent L. Guastalli —

di costituire una regolare Loggia subordinata in Chicago Stato di Illinois sotto il titolo e nome di

Roseland, N. 1723

e di eseguire in essa tutte le cerimonie ed i riti dell'Ordine Figli d'Italia in America, secondo le Leggi ed i Rituali dell'Ordine.

Resta nondimeno convenuto che:

1º La facoltà ed il privilegio di concedere Dispense in qualunque parte degli Stati Uniti di America, suoi Territorii e Dipendenze, appartiene inalterabilmente ed esclusivamente a questa Loggia Suprema;

2º Qualunque Dispensa, già concessa, può essere ritirata ed annullata dalla medesima Loggia Suprema nel caso di disubbidienza o che non siano state osservate le Leggi dell'Ordine.

Noi quindi, Ufficiali autorizzati, confermiamo il nostro consenso per la istituzione della sopradetta Loggia e in fede di ciò rilasciamo ai sunnominati fratelli la presente

DISPENSA

munita del Sigillo della Loggia Suprema dell'Ordine Figli d'Italia in America, e vi apponiamo le nostre firme.

Dato in New York il 15 Agosto 1934

Il Venerabile Supremo

Il Segretario Archivista Supremo

Controfirmato dal Gran Venerabile della Gran Loggia dello Stato di Illinois

Attestato dal Gran Segretario in Chicago il giorno 26 Agosto 1934

Il Gran Venerabile

Il Gran Segretario

FONDATO NEL 1905

This Sons of Italy charter was issued to Alex Adducci, Domenic Lupo, and Vincent Gustalli in 1934 establishing the Roseland Lodge #1723 of OSIA. Founded in 1905, OSIA claims the largest and most dispersed membership of any Italian-American organization in the United States. The organization of this club in Roseland in 1934 is indicative both of the growing Italian nationalism in the 1930s and the fact that Roseland was a committee of "joiners."

Mothers of Italian-American boys in the service were honored at a street corner ceremony in Chicago Heights c. 1943. Many second generation Italian-American men were just the right age for the military draft. Some estimate that about a million Italian Americans served during World War II.

George Spatuzza, depicted here on the cover of a 1941 Dinner Program, was the long time leader of the Sons of Italy. He was among those Italian-American leaders who had to shift gears from working closely with the fascist government of Italy in the 1930s to working actively to bring down the regime in the 1940s. A native of Ragusa, Sicily, Spatuzza did several radio broadcasts to his homeland, encouraging them to welcome the invading American forces.

Among the participants at a meeting to discuss the Sojourn in Italy Program in 1963 are: top left Victor Arrigo, Father Pierini, and Consul General Giovanni Mayr (far right), seated at right is Maurice Marchello. The lecture program drew large audiences.

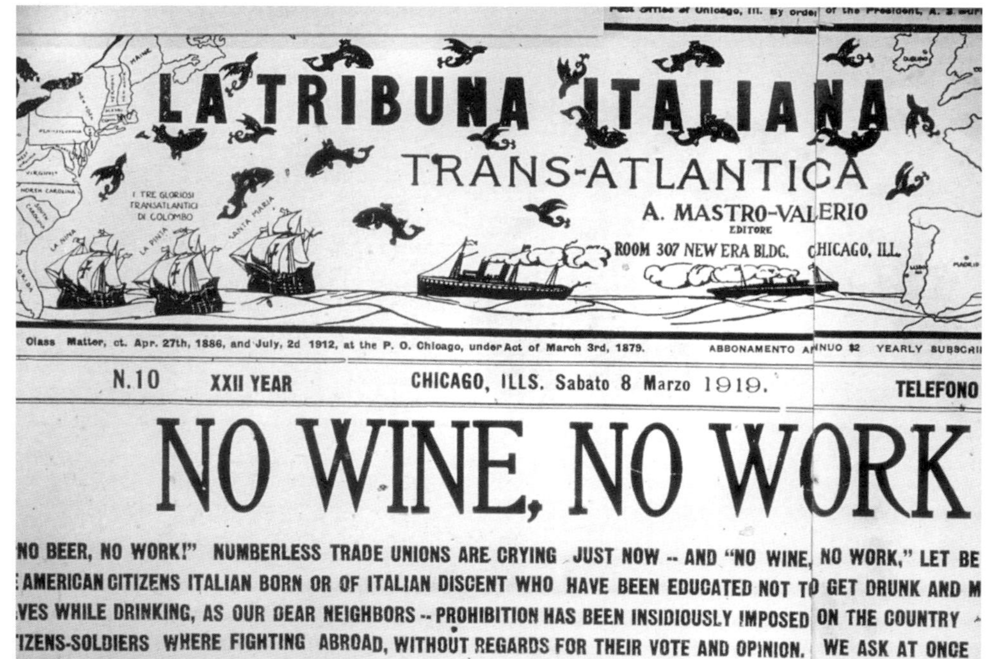

Post Office of Chicago, Ill. By order of the President, A. S. Burl

LA TRIBUNA ITALIANA
TRANS-ATLANTICA

A. MASTRO-VALERIO
EDITORE
ROOM 307 NEW ERA BLDG. CHICAGO, ILL.

I TRE GLORIOSI TRANSATLANTICI DI COLOMBO

Class Matter, ct. Apr. 27th, 1886, and July, 2d 1912, at the P. O. Chicago, under Act of March 3rd, 1879. ABBONAMENTO ANNUO $2 YEARLY SUBSCRI

N.10 XXII YEAR CHICAGO, ILLS. Sabato 8 Marzo 1919. TELEFONO

NO WINE, NO WORK

NO BEER, NO WORK!" NUMBERLESS TRADE UNIONS ARE CRYING JUST NOW -- AND "NO WINE, NO WORK," LET BE
AMERICAN CITIZENS ITALIAN BORN OR OF ITALIAN DISCENT WHO HAVE BEEN EDUCATED NOT TO GET DRUNK AND M
VES WHILE DRINKING, AS OUR DEAR NEIGHBORS -- PROHIBITION HAS BEEN INSIDIOUSLY IMPOSED ON THE COUNTRY
IZENS-SOLDIERS WHERE FIGHTING ABROAD, WITHOUT REGARDS FOR THEIR VOTE AND OPINION. WE ASK AT ONCE
ON THE QUESTION. WE DO NOT WONDER THAT SO MANY ITALIANS ARE RETURNING TO THEIR OLD COUNTRY, DEPRI
AMERICA OF THEIRUSEFUL AND NECESSARY LABOR.

READ IN THE NEXT PAGE THE SPLENDID ARTICLE "FOOD VAL
FESSOR GUIDO ROSSATI, THE MIST EXPERT AND LEARNED JUDG
AND OLIVE OIL

Alessandro Mastro-Valerio's La Tribuna Transatlantica *opposed Prohibition. This 1919 headline and story played on the hope that a general strike by the labor unions would somehow derail the Prohibition Amendment.*

First Lady Pat Nixon and Mayor Richard J. Daley lead the Columbus Day Parade down State Street in the early 1970s. Pictured in the front lines are, from left to right, Governor Dan Walker, Aldermen Vito Marzullo and Fred Roti, businessman Anthony Paterno, County Commissioner Frank Chesrow, and Parade Chair John Porcelli.

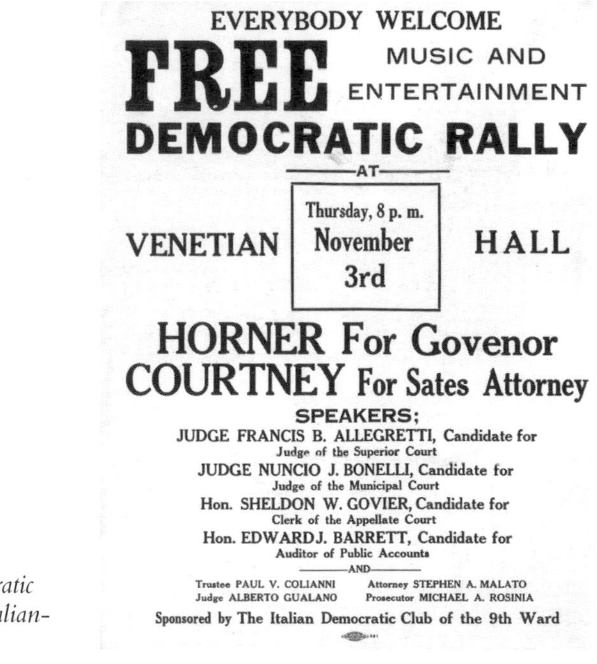

A 1930s flyer from the Italian Democratic club invited Roseland voters to meet Italian-American candidates for judge.

Enrico Fermi was the émigré physicist who at the University of Chicago supervised the first nuclear chain reaction in 1942. This discovery made possible the development of the atomic bomb. The giant FermiLab located west of the city is one of his legacies. It is a constant reminder to the people of Chicago of the great scientific discoveries of this remarkable Italian in Chicago.

Colonel Frank Chesrow at the Army Reserve Camp, a pharmacist, art collector, and explorer, was elected to the Metropolitan Sanitary District and Cook County Board on the Democratic ticket in the period 1948–1966.

In June 1973, friends congratulated Ernie Dalle Molle (center) for his election to the Roseland-Pullman area Sports Hall of Fame. An expert bowler, Dalle Molle also worked hard in the 1930s and 1940s to promote bowling leagues within St. Anthony's Parish. Receiving a check in commemoration of the event is Father Pierini. Far right is Mario Avignone, Fra Noi *"Petals from Roseland" columnist.*

Labor leaders Joseph Signola, James Coli Jr., Joint Civic Committee President Joe Tolitano, Congressman Frank Annunzio, Jerry Cosentino, James Coli Sr., and Congressman Marty Russo pose for a photo at a JCCIA fundraiser honoring Signola. Much of the power of the Italian-American community was rooted in on cooperation between the power bases represented in this picture.

One of the distinctive activities of the Joint Civic Committee is the Italian Heritage Cotillion. This 1977 event was probably presented as a joint venture with the Our Lady of Pompeii Parish.

Jerry Cosentino and the man identified as his mentor, Alderman Vito Marzullo, are at a 1974 fundraiser for Cosentino's successful bid for election to the Metropolitan Sanitary District Board. Cosentino was the first and only Italian-named person elected to a statewide office in Illinois. His ambitions to become governor of Illinois were dashed when a scandal relating to his trucking business was disclosed.

Dominick Di Matteo Sr. and his son built up the Dominick's Grocery business from a single corner store into a 100-store chain. The story of his accomplishments is representative of the success that Italian Americans have had in food-related businesses. "They really know their food."

Music Czar James Caesar Petrillo often created controversy on both the local and national level when he played hard ball on behalf of the American Federation of Musicians.

Devotees gather at St. Mary of Mount Carmel Church, 67th and Hermitage Streets, on September 23, 1903 to celebrate the first feast of San Rocco in Chicago. After the Italian people left the neighborhood in the 1960s the faithful continued the celebration at a variety of locations. It currently takes place at St. Williams Church at 2600 N. Sayre.

This late 1940s promotional photo for the 11-day Italian Festival for some reason featured big straw hats. Proceeds from the city wide event helped build Villa Scalabrini.

Americo Lupi was one of the best known Italian-language broadcasters. Though Italian-language programming was suspended during World War II, Lupi continued his profession in the post-war era.

Mario and Peggy Avignone of Roseland married in 1943 while Mario was still in the service. By some estimates, a million (mostly second generation) Italian Americans served their country during the war and most were considerably Americanized by the experience.

Caricatured on the cover of their 45 r.p.m. record, Gino and Maria Nuccio were post-war migrants to Chicago from Sicily who worked through their radio show, the Italian Radio Theatre, the Fra Noi, *and the Italian Cultural Center to keep an Italian brand of comedy and drama alive.*

Lucy Palermo was the first Italian-American woman elected to the Cook County Board. She served from 1934 to 1938. A product of the Women's Club movement, she focused during wartime on relief for the American prisoners of war in Japan (the Bataan Relief Organization).

VOTE FOR

☒ LUCY PALERMO

Regular Democratic Candidate

—FOR—

County Commissioner

Election, November 6, 1934

83 (OVER)

NOZZE GARFANO—ARMATO

Domenica 4 febbraio prossimo avranno luogo le ben auspicate nozze tra la gentile signorina Pasqua Garfano ed il bravo giovane Giovanni Armato. L'anello nuziale sará benedetto nella chiesa di M. S. di Pompei, McAllister st.

Il ricevimento avrá luogo alle 3 p. m., nella Winchester Hall, 1029 W. Taylor st.

Alla bella coppia, gli auguri di grande felicitá di questa TRIBUNA.

DOPPIE NOZZE

MASTROGIOVANNI-JANNOTTA-GUALANO

Il signore e la signora Modestino Mastrogiovanni ci annunziano gentilmente che le nozze tra le loro figliuole Diana col signor Emilio A. Iannotta e dell'altra loro figliuola Giuditta col signor Ettore J. Gualano J. ebbero luogo il 26 dicembre 1916

Noi auguriamo grandi felicitá alle belle coppie

La Tribuna Transatlantica *published in 1916 these wedding announcements for Pasqua Garfaro and Giovanni Arma, and for Diana Mastrogiovanni and Emilio Janotta. Lavish weddings were a cultural tradition, even among families with limited means. This practice created business opportunities for Italian-American florists, tailors, caterers, jewelers, and photographers.*

Giuseppe Bertelli was the founder of La Parola dei Socialisti *in 1908. He remained an active supporter of socialist causes in Chicago for the next 30 years.*

BRICK SALE TICKETS ARE NOW AVAILABLE

A Chicagoland Community Project

Fr. Pierini and Fr. Cozzi

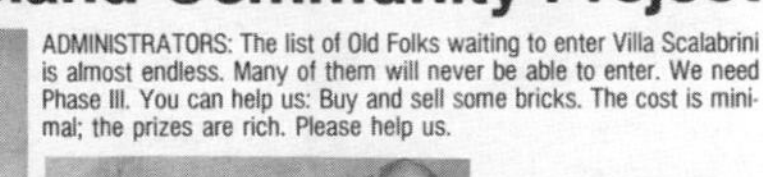

ADMINISTRATORS: The list of Old Folks waiting to enter Villa Scalabrini is almost endless. Many of them will never be able to enter. We need Phase III. You can help us: Buy and sell some bricks. The cost is minimal; the prizes are rich. Please help us.

(L. to r.) Giovanna Inzerillo 93, Rose Lobello 99 and Anselmo Nanni 93.

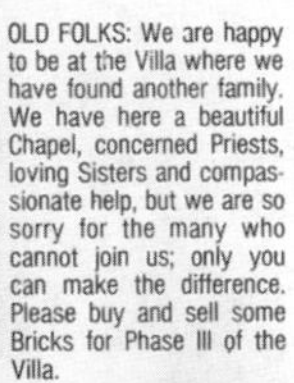

OLD FOLKS: We are happy to be at the Villa where we have found another family. We have here a beautiful Chapel, concerned Priests, loving Sisters and compassionate help, but we are so sorry for the many who cannot join us; only you can make the difference. Please buy and sell some Bricks for Phase III of the Villa.

Sister Julia and Sister Clorinda

SISTERS: We are Scalabrini Sisters and consider it a privilege to serve The Lord in the persons of our Old People. It is heartbreaking to see so many of them rejected for lack of room. We pray that this Brick Sale will give us the help we need.

WORKERS: Our work is not pleasant nor easy, but we do it willingly since we deal directly with our Old Folks. Above all, we remember that Our Lord tells us: What you do for the least of my breathren, you do it for me. Push the Brick Sale. Please give us a generous hand.

Workers Mr. & Mrs. Giacomo Mucia

We're Sending One Brick Sale Book To Each Fra Noi Subscriber. Please Sell It Or Buy It—Return Money And Stubs . . . And Ask For More. Thanks

5 Prizes For Ticket Buyers: $7,000 in Cash
5 Prizes For Ticket Sellers: $1,000 in Cash

A 1970s mailer solicited contributions for phase III of the Villa. By this time the demand for space there had exceeded the supply. This put enormous pressure on the administrators to be fair to both the family members of financial supporters and the general Italian-American public.

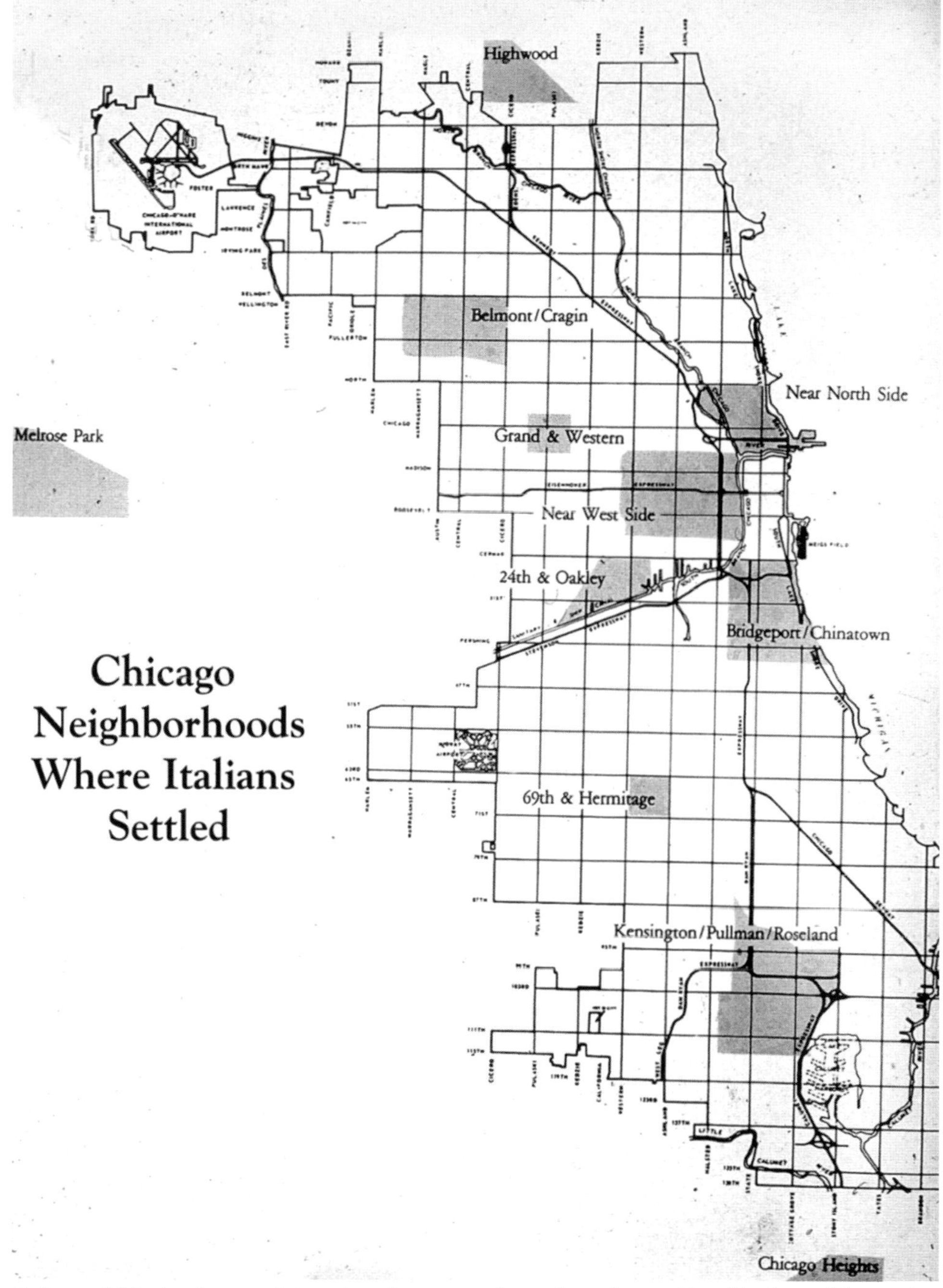

Italian neighborhoods were cloistered on the near north, south, and west sides of the Loop. The coming of expressways, their desire to live in better neighborhoods, and the racial changes in the city that followed World War II brought about the virtual demise of Little Italies in Chicago.

These children are part of one of the many divisions of the Santissima Maria Lauretana Society.

EVERYBODY WELCOME!

GRAND CELEBRATION
15th Anniversary of the Italian Armistice Day Sat. Nov. 4th, 1933

SPONSORED BY THE
Federation of the Italian World War Veterans in the United States of America, Inc.

PROGRAM

Parade will start at 3:30 P. M. from the Italian Legion Headquarters 2106 W. Lake Street and will proceed to Veterans Field Auditorium, N. 16th Ave. and Hirsh St., Melrose Park

American Legion Drum and Bugle Corps, Post 133
American Legion Post 133 of Maywood.
American Legion Drums and Bugle Corps, Post 368
American Legion Sarlo-Sharp Post 368
Italian Legion of Chicago
Italian Legion of Joliet
San Michele Arcangelo Lodge of Melrose Park
Benjamin Franklin Lodge No. 37 I. A. N. U.
San Giuseppe Lodge No. 50 I. A. N. U. Melrose Pk.
V. Dabormida Lodge No. 9 I. A. N. U. Melrose Pk.
Aso Appennini Lodge of Melrose Park
Indipendenza Italiana Lodge of Melrose Park
Maria Santissima Misericordia Lodge of Melrose
Liberty Buster Club of Melrose Park
Union Social Club of Melrose Park
Duca degli Abbruzzi Lodge of Melrose Park
Italian Legion Auxiliary No. 5 of Melrose Park
Italian Legion Band of Melrose Park
Hon. Joseph Imburgio President of Melrose Park
Royal Italian Consulate General Cav. Uff. Giuseppe Castruccio, Hon. Louis Senese Jr., Lt. John Rossi, Hon. Michael Sorviello, Hon. Peter di Francesca.
Italian Legion of Melrose Park, Illinois

Nick Zullo and Bruno Bros. will sing Italian and American Songs

Free Dance **Music by the Italian Legion Orchestra**

Everybody Welcome to the Veteran's Field Auditorium

This invitation to an Armistice Day event in Melrose Park lists five "Italian Legion" and four American Legion posts expected to be in attendance. Apparently a significant number of veterans of the Italian Army ("Ex-Combattenti") in World War I had organized clubs in Joliet, Chicago, and Melrose Park. Also in attendance were Italian Consul General Giuseppe Castruccio, Judge Louis Senese, and Joseph Imburgio, the mayor of Melrose Park.

Many Italian-American women worked at candy factories. Here, the women of Brach's mug for the camera in the late 1930s.

This photo tells the story of neighborhood change on the near north side in the late 1950s and early 1960s when most of the neighborhood had been demolished to make way for Cabrini-Green Public Housing. The organizers of the Lauretana feast attempted to improvise. They erected steel poles and guide wire to recreate the flight of the angels, which had always taken place from one three flat to another three flat across the street.

A fire destroyed Santa Maria Addolorata Church at Peoria and Grand in 1931, leaving the Pugliese and Sicilian families temporarily without a church.

This picture shows the bar at the Del Rio Restaurant in Highwood in the 1930s. For three generations the same family has run this well known restaurant.

Crowd estimates varied between 60,000 and 100,000 for the Soldier Field reception for General Balbo in July 1933. This was the single proudest day in the history of Italians in Chicago.

The Michigan Avenue Commercial strip in Roseland in the 1940s did vibrant business and inspired in the St. Anthony parishioners high optimism. Some of the businesses depicted in the photo are Roseland Recreation and Billiards, the Roseland Theatre, Jostes Sporting Goods, a candy store, a liquor store, and much more.

...SPRING DANCE...

Featuring LOUIS PANICO AND HIS N. B. C. RADIO BAND

GIVEN BY ROSELAND DECAGONS

FRI. EVE., APRIL 14TH, 1939

VENETIAN BALLROOM, 139 KENSINGTON AVE. ROSELAND

ENTREE 8:30 P. M. ADMISSION 35c

Louis Panico learned to play the trumpet at Hull House and in the 1920s became the best known trumpet soloist in the county for his "laughing" trumpet. In 1939 he appeared with his NBC band at Roseland's Venetian Ballroom.

The author's father, Lodovico Candeloro, hangs braids of onions and garlic in his grape arbor in Chicago Heights in the 1980s. Large gardens provided immigrants with economic, gastronomic, and psychic benefits and allowed them to maintain their ethnicity by continuing to "eat Italian."

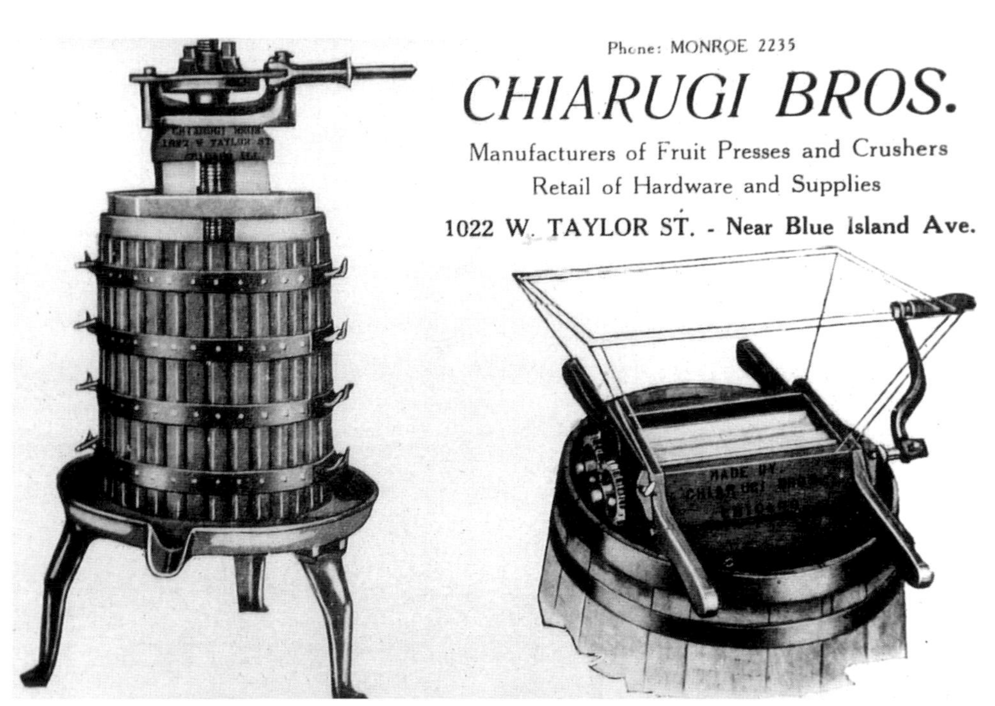

Machines like these, made and sold by Chiarugi Brothers at 1022 W. Taylor, brought wine making into the reach of thousands of Italians in Chicago before, during, and after the Prohibition Era.

Societé di mutuo soccorso *were especially important when there was a death in the family. These items are momentos of a bygone era.*

The current Dell'Alpe Italian Foods (Rubinelli, Inc.) got its start at 804 W. Randolph, near the corner of Randolph and Halsted. Pictured above are Barney Rubinelli and Frank Bertacci in front of the store in the 1930s. The family hailed from Borga Manero, near Torino, and came first to work in the coal mines of Southern Illinois. Typical of Italian businesses in Chicago, Robert Rubinelli, the current CEO, is the third generation of his family to run the business.

Like this man, Italian immigrants were mostly contadini *(small farmers). Their adjustment to crowded urban slums in Chicago was not an easy one.*

Ann Sufretini-Sassetti is the only woman ever to preside over the Italian American Chamber of Commerce of Chicago. In this photo, Sassetti presents an award to Robert Marcucci in honor of the 100th anniversary of the Gonnella Baking Company.

Queen Isabella and Cristoforo Colombo wave from their float in a 1980s Columbus Day Parade.

The Italian American Chamber of Commerce Bolletino *celebrated the end of Prohibition with the cartoon showing legal beer as the prodigal son returning home to "Common Sense."*

BOLLETTINC)I COMMERCIO ITALIANA 11

Il Ritorno del Figliuol Prodigo

Pubblichiamo il "Cartoon" del ritorno della birra al "Buon Senso" perchè quando dalla Proibizione viene tolta l'aureola di puritanesimo dalla quale nacque, non resta che una vera stonatura contro il buon senso. La birra e i vini, che da anni sono trovati nelle mani del commercio illegale, presto saranno ritornati al giusto loro posto, ad un commercio fiorente e onorato.

The most important business association for Italians in Chicago was the Italian American Chamber of Commerce. Founded in 1907 by Cuneos and other old line importers, the Chamber network aided the food importers and it provided a conduit to the larger business environment in Chicago. Pictured above is a 1912 banquet in honor of a delegation of visiting Italian businessmen.

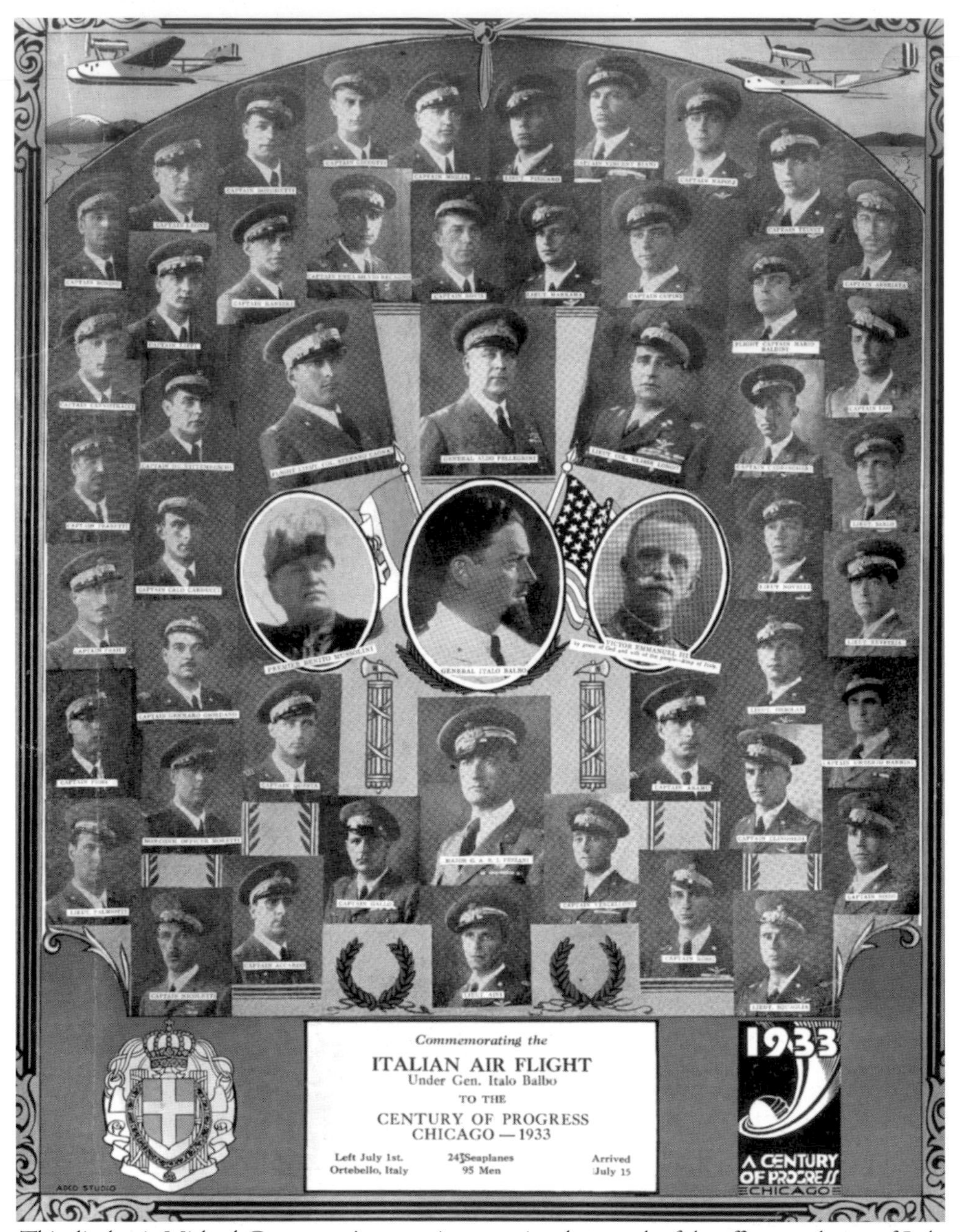

This display is Michael Castronova's souvenir composite photograph of the officers and crew of Italo Balbo's Trans-Oceanic flight to Chicago's Century of Progress Fair in 1933. Note the presence of Fascist symbols and the photos of Mussolini and King Victor Emanuel II.

Mike Pupillo's poolroom in the west grand avenue neighborhood was typical of the 1930s era. Frank Pupillo, Joseph Cirignani (1915–1985), Artie (last name unknown), and Patrick Cirignani (1916–1990) apparently played pool in an unheated room. They have their gloves and coats on. Joe and Patrick were brothers. The owner Mike Pupillo lived 1899–1973 and was from Carbonara di Bari, Puglia.

The Maroons soccer team had its origins in the 1920s. Over the years, the powerful bonds of sport and ethnicity have expanded the scope of the Maroons to include soccer programs for boys and girls of all ages. The Maroons also function as a very active social club from their headquarters near Grand and Harlem in Elmwood Park.

Vito Tunzi was one of the thousands of Chicago Italians who served in the military in the 1940s. Shown here in his Army Air Corp flight uniform, Tunzi hailed from Fluornoy and Western.

Antonio Paris, Sidney Misrac, an unidentified clerk, Mr. Giuliano, and Frank Paris pose in front of Paris and Giuliano Imports on the southwest corner of Taylor and Halsted in the heart of the Near West Side Little Italy, 1931. In the display windows are mountains of spaghetti, olive oil, cheese, and wine products. Within a quarter mile of this place were hundreds of Italian businesses and the Maxwell Street Market area.

A little bit of clout on the part of State Representative Ralph Capparelli (far right) helped get this sign erected on the Eisenhower Expressway in the early 1980s. Joining him in celebrating this increased visibility for the Italian Cultural Center are Tony Sorrentino, Father Roberto Simionato, director of the center, and Leonora LiPuma, champion volunteer on behalf of the center.

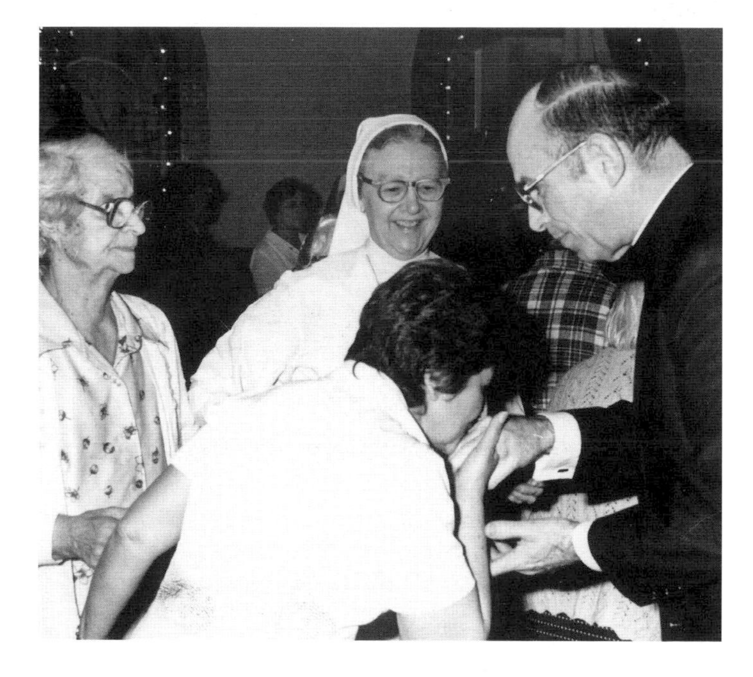

For a short time Cardinal Bernardin's mother was a resident at the Villa Scalabrini and he visited often. On this visit in 1982, residents and staff lined up to kiss the Cardinal's ring.

Two controversial Italian American Teamster Union leaders, Jimmy Hoffa and Joseph Glimco Sr. (head of Local 777 cab drivers) raise their arms in victory in the late 1950s. Glimco and other Chicago Teamsters gave key support to Hoffa's successful bid for the International Presidency of the Teamsters.

The ability of Italian produce and beverage importers to supply the immigrant colonies with Italian staples and delicacies produced the first successful businesses within the group. An example of the way that Rubinelli Importers created a niche within the Italian-American market is this 1920s label for Dell'Alpe brand Tamarindo syrup. Not much used today, tamarind syrup, diluted and mixed with fresh lemons and ice, made a perfect summer cooler.

Continued from page 64
(except for the West Side Bloc). This group of Republicans had an uncanny record of "surprising" everyone by voting with the Kelly (later Daley) machine Democrats on key issues from the 1940s–1960s. Suburban Italian-named politicos tend to be Republican, while downstate Illinois seems to produce Democratic leaders.

Not much is known about the first Italian Chicago aldermen, Stephen Rovere, who served on the city council from 1885 to 1897, or Frank Gazzolo (1892–1913). Schiavo lists Frank Brignadello, Stephen Malato, and William Navigato as elected state representatives in the 1890s. Italian immigrant voters seemed to ignore the local recommendations of the two prominent Italian-American journalists of the era, Alessandro Masto-Valerio (*La Tribuna Transatlantica*) and Oscar Durante (*L'Italia*) who were allies of Jane Addams and her circle of reformers in the West Side Italian neighborhood. Instead, Italian voters supported bosses like Irishman Johnny Powers (Gianni di Paoli to Italian speakers) in return for minor patronage jobs and municipal services packaged as political favors.

In his upbeat 1928 analysis of Italian politics in Chicago, Schiavo claimed that the group was "beginning to climb the ladder." He then proceeded to list a dozen office holders including State Senator James Leonardo, State Representatives Joseph Perina, Charles Cioa, Michael Durso, Aldermen A.J. Prignano and William Pacelli, City Sealer Daniel Serritella, Chief Clerk in the prosecutor's office, Peter Granata, and Board of Improvements member James Vignola as men with a future. But Schiavo reserved his highest accolades for former Judge Bernard Barasa, "the leading Italian in politics in Chicago." Though he ran unsuccessfully in mayoral and county primaries in the early 1920s, Barasa never achieved the success that Schiavo had predicted for him. Serritella, on the other hand, became ward committeeman and a powerful state senator from the First District. Granata later became one of the West Side Bloc. Both Serritella and Granata ended up with besmirched reputations.

Humbert Nelli describes the rough and tumble struggle of colorful Anthony D'Andrea, president of the mostly Italian Hod Carriers' Union and the Unione Siciliana. D'Andrea was a defrocked priest, a red light district impresario, and a convicted counterfeiter. Though he and Powers had a truce in 1920, it fell apart and D'Andrea decided to run against 19th Ward Alderman Powers in 1921. Typical of the era, the campaign featured political bombings, feuds among Italians who supported rival candidates, kidnappings, and fist fights. Despite his ability and willingness to fight fire with fire, D'Andrea lost to the "Prince of the Boodlers" by 389 votes. In May 1921 D'Andrea was dead, the victim of a shotgun attack.

To avoid this kind of embarrassing challenge in the future, Powers and the council majority increased the number of wards from 35 to 50, making sure to gerrymander the Italian vote in Ward 19, where it was a majority, into four different wards, where Italians were in the minority. It was only through the efforts of Al Capone later in the decade that Italians were able to capture full political power on the Near West Side.

In contrast to Schiavo, Nelli's analysis of Italian-American political figures in the 1920s portrays the group as pals of Al Capone. Nelli and Capone biographer John Kobler contend that by the mid-1920s, Big Al was the most powerful Italian-American political figure in the city and people like Serritella, Granata, Pacelli, Prignano, and Roland Libonati (pictured in the Schiavo book) were Capone cronies.

No discussion of Italian Americans in politics would be complete without some discussion of the city's most famous Italian American, Al Capone.

The image of this gangster who for 20 years operated a vice, gambling, and illegal liquor empire under the bribed consent of the city's non-Italian political leadership has besmirched the name not only of Italians in Chicago, but of the city itself. The universal reaction in any foreign land to the announcement that one is from Chicago is the rat-tat-tat of the machine gun and the knowing mention of the most notorious gangster in world history. The legacy of this plague of lawlessness has been extensive. Hundreds of innocent neighborhood people of all ages were terrorized into distorted and cynical attitudes about law and order. Most important has been the criminal image of Italians, which non-Italians have held and non-Sicilians have developed of Sicilians within the city.

There is more. Capone and his kind had an economic impact on the Italian community. Sociologist Daniel Bell has dubbed it the "queer ladder to success" and sociologist Francis Ianni has detailed the allure that organized crime has had for underprivileged ethnics as an avenue of social mobility. The exploits of the Genna brothers and the 42 gang on the West Side were described by John Landesco in *Organized Crime in Chicago* (1929). Landesco saw this type of criminality as rooted in the social disorganization of the neighborhood rather than a cultural legacy of immigrants. Humbert Nelli, in outlining the integration of organized crime in the political and economic structure of Chicago, has emphasized that the members of criminal syndicates were American-born practitioners of the American ethic of success at any cost: "Turning to crime was not a denial of the American way of life, but rather comprised an effort by common laborers who lacked skills to find 'success.' They used the most readily available means at their disposal." The title of one of Nelli's books says it all—*The Business of Crime.*

Nelli further points out that Chicago politicians had been using underworld elements to win elections long before Italians came to the city. Though the numbers directly involved in syndicate crime were less than one percent of the Italian American people, the Capone mob did share some of its wealth by employing compatriots and relatives for both the legal and illegal aspects of their business. A showoff, Capone fancied himself a Robin Hood, passing out cash at social functions and establishing soup kitchens for the destitute during the Depression. Many of his associates used their ill-gotten fortunes as a base to launch subsequent generations into the professions. Others simply launched future generations into the same kind of business, bequeathing the Italian community a substratum of organized crime that to this day lurks in and out of political activities, affecting both the Italian and the larger communities. The concern, even among Italian Americans, that some of the ethnic leaders asking for their support just might be "connected," sows seeds of distrust in the community and undermines attempts to unify the group.

Organized crime and elected officials have a natural affinity. Candidates need campaign funds and volunteers while businessmen who deal in illicit commodities like bootleg liquor, gambling, and prostitution need elected officials to "look the other way" and apply lax enforcement of the laws concerning their commercial activities. Capone's business of "Giving the people what they want" required an aggressive "governmental relations" policy. Add to that situation the universal unpopularity in Chicago of the Prohibition law and the fact that some Italian-American political figures had grown up with (or were related to) organized crime functionaries, and you get a formula for undermining the credibility of Italian-American office seekers. The stereotype has dogged ambitious Italian Americans since that era.

Regarding Capone's political influence, Kobler presents evidence that Serritella served as Capone's agent in the city council in the 1920s. Capone and other organized crime leaders helped engineer the mayoral victory of Bill Thompson over incumbent William Dever. From 1923 to 1927 Dever waged a sincere battle to enforce Prohibition as the law of the land and had been so successful that Capone was forced to move his operations outside the city limits for a time. But Thompson, who described himself as "wet as the Atlantic Ocean," promised a wide open town with 10,000 new speakeasies.

Needless to say, Capone and his rival bootleggers jumped heavily onto Thompson's bandwagon. Capone reportedly used every technique of bribery and terrorism on behalf of Thompson, and Kobler credits the gangster with coining the slogan "Vote early and vote often" in this 1927 election, proving once again that "Chicago politics ain't bean bag." Big Bill's electoral victory created a situation in which Capone claimed to have half the Chicago Police Department on his payroll and to have thousands of Italian immigrant families producing illicit beverages to satisfy millions of thirsty Chicagoans—exaggerations, no doubt, that capture the truth. Unfortunately, Thompson's non-enforcement policy also led to increased competition among the bootleggers that escalated into widespread violence, the most spectacular example of which is the St. Valentine's Day Massacre.

Typical of the Italian-American politicians in the 1920s was "The Diamond"—Joe Esposito, First Ward committeeman. Joe Diamond had style. He was an impeccable dresser with glittering diamonds on both hands. He ran the Bella Napoli restaurant and during the 1924 Presidential campaign would go from table to table urging his Italian patrons to "Keep a da cool with Mr. Cool [Coolidge]." He very effectively used his restaurant to do favors for his many friends and supporters and he never missed a wake or a wedding. Poor Italian mothers could count on Diamond Joe for a $10 handout if things really got tough. He was godfather (*padrino*) to dozens of boys and *compare* to hundreds of their parents.

According to Maurice Marchello in his *Crossing the Tracks*, "It was the custom in those days for Italian-American politicians to request their local mayor, governors and senators . . . to become godparents of their children. . . . Senator Charles Deneen was a 'Compare' to Da Diamond and many others." And Diamond Joe was, in turn, the godfather of many young men as well. When one of them, a young lawyer, came to Esposito for help after being rejected for a job in U.S. District Attorney Johnson's office, Diamond Joe consoled him, "Comparuccio Mio [my dear little godson], don'ta you worry. I feexa dat dumb Swede Johnson. Get Senatore Deneen on da phone righta now!" Marchello continued the story, "Following the lengthy phone conversation, replete with the choicest swearwords, Diamond finally put the receiver down, embraced his godson-lawyer and said: She'sa all feexed up. No more worry. You start next week!" In the late 1920s, Diamond Joe was murdered, apparently by gangsters. His funeral was one of the most lavish in Chicago history, in keeping with his high style.

Thus, the Italian-American electorate and political leadership was schooled in a milieu in which bossism triumphed over Jane Addams's reformism, one in which non-Italian bosses were often the best sources for patronage jobs, and in an atmosphere where most political campaigns were characterized by violence, intimidation, and hooliganism. The practical reality of this era is that almost all politicians of whatever ethnicity were corrupt. Italian Americans in the late 1920s did not need Sacco-Vanzetti or Mussolini's American Fascist movement to make them (confused) cynics. Better to focus on honest work and family affairs.

It is with this dubious heritage that Italian Americans moved into the second half of the century. The soldiers came home from military service, the population moved to the suburbs, and the working class generation was succeeded by a better-educated, more middle-class cohort. This Italian segment of the "Greatest Generation" in the last part of the century faced additional demands from African Americans and Latinos for their share of the pie. The success of African Americans in getting elected as mayor, Cook County board president, and U.S. senator in the 1980s and 1990s only increased the frustration level of the Euro-Ethnics.

The general pattern for Italian-American political achievement in the two decades after World War II was for a half dozen Italians to be elected to the Chicago City Council (out of 50) from the wards in which they could find some Italian base. Some of those same districts and the Proviso Township (Melrose Park) and the Chicago Heights areas generally elected a handful of Italian Americans to Springfield. It continued to be an era when candidates, officeholders, and patronage workers had to have a "sponsor." As the writer Milton Rakove brilliantly put it, "Don't make no waves. Don't back no losers." This could have been the slogan for two generations of savvy machine operatives who knew how to take care of themselves and their relatives. Occasionally Italian-American aldermen got caught up in the periodic corruption investigations that are a staple of Chicago politics.

All Chicago politics is based on place and influence. The one time that an Italian issue did emerge in the 1960s—when Mayor Richard J. Daley decided to tear down the Italian neighborhood to make way for the University of Illinois at Chicago—the Italian elected officials rolled over and played dead, leaving only a heroic housewife, Florence Scala, to lead a fruitless battle to save the Near West Side Italian community. In fact, when the north side Sicilian neighborhood was programmed for public housing (Cabrini-Green), there was even less resistance.

The most colorful of Chicago Italian politicians, Vito Marzullo, became a precinct captain in 1920, was elected state representative in 1940, and became alderman from the near Southwest Side 25th Ward (that included the 24th and Oakley neighborhood) in 1953. Fiercely loyal to the Democratic machine, Marzullo put into practice the maxim that "all politics is local politics." He was a powerful ally of the first Mayor Daley and in the 1980s was referred to as the dean of city council. He was lionized at Harvard University, where he lectured to a political science class in non-standard English. And he resented criticism from reformers and the media. As he put it:

> I ain't got no axes to grind. You can take all your news media and all the do-gooders in town and move them into my 25th Ward, and do you know what would happen? On election day we'd beat you fifteen to one. The mayor don't run the 25th Ward, Neither does the news media or the do-gooders. Me, Vito Marzullo. that's who runs the 25th Ward, and on election day everybody does what Vito Marzullo tells them.

Totally in control of the 25th and focused only on the 25th, Marzullo unconsciously symbolized the limited ambitions of his generation of ethnic politicians. As Sam Smith has explained in *Shadows of Hope*:

> In the world of Plunkitt and Marzullo politics was not something handed down to the people through such intermediaries as Larry King. It was not the product of spin doctors, campaign hired guns or phony town meetings. It welled up from the bottom, starting with one loyal follower, one ambitious ballplayer, twelve unhappy pushcart peddlers. What defined politics was an unbroken chain of human experience, memory and gratitude.

In a period when hardly anyone knew who was on the Cook County Board of Commissioners, the Democrats nominated and elected Lucy Russo Palermo and Peter Fosco. In 1934, two weeks before the election, the Kelly-Nash machine called on Palermo, who was elected and served one term. Lucy Russo Palermo (1885–1979) has the distinction of being the first Italian-American woman elected to public office in the history of Chicago. Throughout the 1920s and 1930s she was president of the American Italian Federated Club—affiliated with the Chicago Cook County Federation of Women's Clubs. They engaged in charity work, eventually focusing on helping the patients at the Oak Forest Hospital.

During that era, Palermo collected a scrapbook full of memories: the governor chose her as a host for the World's Fair, she was part of the committee that organized a 1935 dinner at the Saddle and Cycle Club for President and Mrs. Roosevelt, she helped establish the first blood bank at Cook County Hospital, and she had the opportunity to mobilize large numbers of volunteers to help improve the conditions at Oak Forest Hospital. A reported squabble with the Kelly-Nash leaders got her dropped from the 1938 Democratic slate, but she resurfaced in 1942 with an unsuccessful bid for state representative. After her term in office, she joined the Mothers, Mobilize for America, an isolationist group which opposed the country's involvement in World War II. Since the Mothers group was considered pro-Axis, Palermo was brought before a grand jury but subsequently not charged. After the start of the war, she turned her attention to organizing relief for the American POWs who had been captured when American forces were defeated in the Philippines at Bataan. One of her sons was among the POWs. In the early 1950s she moved to Tuscon, where she ran for county supervisor at age 86 in 1971.

Fosco was a powerful First Ward committeeman from 1938 to 1951, destined to become the leader of the Laborers' International Union. His service on the county board lasted from 1938 to 1946, raising the possibility that he replaced Palermo in the "Italian seat" on the board.

Frank Chesrow (Cesario) (1903–1989) was a second generation Calabrian. According to legend, Jane Addams somehow suggested to Chesrow's family that the name Cesario might be changed to Chesrow. In any case, Chesrow received a pharmacy degree from Valparaiso University and became a sanitary engineer in the army. In 1943, he was assigned to America's occupation forces battling typhus in Naples. He later became a liaison officer between the U.S. military and the Italian Army and the Italian Government.

In 1948, Chesrow won a seat on the Metropolitan Sanitary District Board, becoming the president of that body from 1958 to 1966. In a statement that might seem strange coming from a political figure supported by the Cook County Democratic Machine, he stated, "We reduced our budget 32% in the period 1961–1966 without curtailing operations. In fact, we handled the equivalent of a million more people with less money and less personnel." Chesrow was an art collector and served for a time as the president of the Municipal Art League. He was a Papal Chamberlain in Pope John XXIII's retinue. In 1970, he got the nod from Democratic slatemakers for a slot on the Cook County Board where he served until 1986. His brother Eugene, a physician, also worked for Cook County as director of the Oak Forest Hospital.

Roland Libonati in 1957 became the first Illinois Italian American elected to the U.S. Congress when he was chosen in a mid-term election in the 7th District (Central Chicago and the West Side). A veteran member of the West Side Bloc in the Illinois House and Senate, Libonati's Democratic seat was passed on to Frank Annunzio in 1964. And on the state level, Senator Peter Granata continued into the early 1960s to reign as chief of the West Side Bloc.

The two most significant and enduring factors in Italian-American political circles in the last half of the century were the Joint Civic Committee of Italian Americans (JCCIA) and the Justinian Society (Italian American Lawyers). The JCCIA was founded in 1952 in response to the Republican State Central Committee's removal of Emil Caliendo, a candidate for municipal judge, from their ticket because of widespread publicity about the "gangland" murder of ward politician Charles Gross. Though no one suggested that this event or other recent "Mafia" activity in the city had anything specifically to do with Caliendo, the Republicans apparently determined that, under the circumstances, it was best not to slate an Italian. On a parallel front, an organization called the Citizens of Greater Chicago launched a campaign to eradicate organized crime in which they appeared to equate "organized crime" with "Italian organized crime."

A hue and cry arose among Italians against this "guilt by association," which prompted the Italian Welfare Council to invite leaders of Italian organizations to a Sunday afternoon meeting at its offices at 20 E. Jackson. The city-wide fledgling organization that emerged was made up of leaders from 50 different Italian American clubs. The group selected Joseph Barbera, an articulate Loop attorney, as its president. Under his leadership, the ad hoc committee convinced the State Republican Committee to reinstate Caliendo. Members of the newly-organized Joint Civic Committee were pleasantly surprised to find that they could get results when they spoke with a unified voice. Thus began the work of the officially non-partisan umbrella organization that became the official voice of the Italian-American community of Chicago.

Under the guidance of Anthony Sorrentino (who served as executive director into the 1980s), and a series of well known attorneys, businessmen, and labor leaders who served as presidents, the JCCIA became an arbiter of culture, prestige, and honor within the Italian community. And it continued to act as the champion of the Italian-American reputation against those who would defame it. When the press or political leaders needed to touch base with the Italian Americans, they contacted the JCCIA. Sorrentino has recorded the history of the JCCIA in his *Organizing the Ethnic Community* (1995).

By the mid-1960s the JCCIA was working closely with newly-elected congressman Frank Annunzio. The dominant political figure among Chicago Italians from the 1960s to the 1990s was Democratic Congressman Frank Annunzio. Annunzio began his career in the mid-1930s as a business arts and history teacher. He later became the legislative and educational director of the Steel Workers Union, and then director of the Illinois Department of Labor in the administration of Governor Adlai Stevenson. In the later 1950s, he played an important part in the JCCIA campaign to support the Villa Scalabrini, bringing together the two most dynamic groups in the city. The personal alliance between Annunzio and Father Armando Pierini was a powerful and a lasting one.

In the 1964 Lyndon Johnson landslide, Annunzio was elected to Congress from the 7th District, succeeding Roland Libonati. In Washington, Annunzio successfully fashioned for himself the role of "leading Italian-American Congressman." He was a major protagonist in getting Columbus Day proclaimed a national holiday. He spearheaded earthquake relief funding for Italy in 1978, and he used his influence to promote the fledgling Washington-based National Italian American Foundation. He was the champion fundraiser for Villa Scalabrini and for the Joint Civic Committee, and he was responsible each year for attracting a top political celebrity to be the grand marshal in Chicago's Columbus Day Parade. As a member of the House Banking Committee, Annunzio championed the rights of the consumers against abuses by credit card companies. He served until 1993, when old age and redistricting hastened his retirement.

For a while, from 1975 to 1993, there were two Italian-American Chicago congressman. Liberal Democrat Marty Russo was a younger man than Annunzio with a more "modern" political style. Representing a mostly white, but ethnically mixed, South and Southwest Suburban District, Russo won a seat on the Ways and Means Committee and struggled with budget and health care issues. He did not make a major issue out of his Italian-American identity. In appearances before the Italian-American community in Chicago, he, of course, deferred to Annunzio. With redistricting in 1992, Russo was defeated in the primary election by fellow incumbent Democratic Congressman William Lipinski, a darling of the machine. Russo eventually became a high powered Washington lobbyist.

For the first time in 30 years, Illinois Italians were without a congressman to call their own until Republican Donald Mazullo of Rockford was elected a few years later. Mazullo, however, seems much less interested in pursuing an ethnic agenda than his Italian-American predecessors.

The Justinian Society is also a major player in the Italian-American political arena. An active fraternity of Italian-American lawyers whose roots go back to the 1920s, its membership has at times reached as high as 1,500. Candidates for public office often look to friends and associates in the Justinian Society to gain access to Italian-American voters. In turn, the leadership of the Justinians has vigilantly monitored judicial appointments and other political appointments on the city, county, and state levels for almost a century.

Sometimes the society has been so successful that Italian names seem to be over-represented in the judiciary. This is a result of several factors. There are thousands of Italian-American lawyers in the city, and every one wants to be a judge. Constitutionally, judges in Illinois are elected, but many judicial careers begin with appointments to mid-term vacancies. Lobbying by the Justinian Society and other intermediaries has often produced favorable results. Moreover, the judiciary offers a political career without the necessity of enduring an all-out political campaign and the inevitable Mafia smears and innuendoes that are mounted against any candidate with an Italian name.

On the other hand, in recent judicial elections, many experienced, well-respected Italian-American judges have been knocked off by unknowns with Irish names. It is clear that when the voting public is confronted with choosing names on a ballot of candidates who are unknown to them, Irish names are more appealing than Italian, Hispanic, or Polish names. In fact, judicial candidates have been known to change their names to acceptable Irish ones to get elected. Though none serve at present, several Italian Americans have sat on the state appellate court, and only one, Moses Harrison III of Carlinville, has ever been elected to the Illinois Supreme Court.

The post-war era also saw the emergence of a new independent brand of Italian-American politician. Closely in touch with his Italian roots, Anthony Scariano became one of the most accomplished Italian Americans in the state. Born in 1918, he grew up in the North Side Sicilian neighborhood. His development was influenced by the Chicago Commons Settlement House. In the late 1930s and early 1940s, Scariano attended George Washington University. During World War II he was recruited into the OSS, the forerunner of the CIA. His undercover work in Northern Italy and Naples during the war was featured in Stud Terkel's *The Good War*. After serving in the OSS, Scariano worked his way through Georgetown Law School by serving as a guard at the Capitol building and later as assistant to Illinois Senator Scott Lucas.

Scariano moved to Park Forest, opened a law practice in Chicago Heights, and was elected to the Illinois State House of Representatives as a Democrat in 1956.

He distinguished himself in the legislature as a champion of education and of the Open Meetings Act. Scariano was so popular with educators and labor unionists that in the 1964 "Bedsheet Ballot," in which all 236 state representative candidates ran statewide for 177 seats, he ran third.

He served in the Illinois House until 1973 when he was appointed to the Illinois Racing Board by maverick Governor Dan Walker. Previously a critic of the board, Scariano is generally credited with reforming the operation that had been plagued by scandals. In 1985, Scariano was appointed to the Illinois Appellate Court and elected in his own right to a ten year term in 1986. After a distinguished career on the bench, he retired in December 1996, at the height of his prestige among Italians and non-Italians in the state. He speaks perfect Italian and Sicilian and is one of the founding members of the Sicilian American Cultural Association (SACA). He currently writes a *Fra Noi* column on the origins and meanings of Italian names.

Scariano has often spoken of his frustration with the bossism of Mayor Richard J. Daley and of his embarrassment with the antics of his West Side Bloc legislative colleagues. If there were a figure whose advancement would have uplifted the reputation of Italian-American politicians, it was Scariano. But his liberalism and his independence won him more favor with journalists and the progressive elements of the Democratic Party than it did with the regular party slatemakers. He was especially shunned by the party regulars for his vote (with the Republicans) for a statewide grand jury to investigate organized crime. Readers can find more information and photos relating to Scariano in the author's *Voices of America: Italians in Chicago.*

Coming out of the same geographic area as Scariano, another "modern" political figure of similar campaigning style, but of different politics, was Republican State Senator Aldo DeAngelis. The son of Marchegiani immigrants, DeAngelis was elected to the Illinois Senate in 1978 where his business background, personal skills, and liberal Republicanism (he supported John Kennedy in 1960) made him so popular on both sides of the aisle that he was quickly brought into the leadership circle. Renowned for his ability to bring state funds to public projects within his district, DeAngelis was honored on the national level with an appointment by President Reagan to the Columbus Quincentenary Committee in the late 1980s. In 1990, he ran for the presidency of the Cook County Board, a post traditionally dominated by Democrats. Despite his pleasing personality and a vigorous campaign, the senator was defeated. And though he lost by a wide margin, the candidate attributed a good part of his deficit to the unacceptability on the county level of his ballot name, with both "Aldo" and "De Angelis" being unmistakably Italian.

Changing demographics and a highly-spirited campaign by newcomer Debbie DeFrancesco Halvorson defeated DeAngelis in his bid for reelection as state senator in 1996. Nevertheless, De Angelis continues to wield power in his new role in Springfield as a legislative lobbyist for some of the largest interest groups in the state of Illinois.

In the post-war era, only one woman, Theresa Petrone, emerged as an enduring political force. The wife of a county judge from a political family on the Near North Side, Petrone was a long-term appointed member and sometime chair of the Illinois State Board of Elections. A quick perusal of state Blue Books (biannual directories of elected and appointed officials) revealed that several females from downstate served briefly as state representatives, sometimes assuming the unexpired term of their deceased spouse. Otherwise, this writer is unaware of female Italian-American elected officials with a significant and enduring power base.

In 1978, the first Italian American was nominated by a major party for statewide office. As related in a 1992 *Tribune* article by Bill Brashler, Jerry Cosentino (1932–1997) grew up in the Bridgeport neighborhood, the 11th of 12 children of an immigrant fresco maker. A high school drop out turned truck driver, Cosentino started his own business with a $700 truck in 1959. By 1970, Fast Motor Freight boasted over 100 trucks in its fleet. In that year, he took an unsuccessful fling at running against the Daley-endorsed congressional candidate in the Summit area. He came so close that his bid two years later for a spot on the Metropolitan Sanitary District Board drew the support of Vito Marzullo, who became his mentor. Cosentino won that election by 400,000 votes. Then in 1978 he was slated and elected state treasurer by a margin of over 150,000 votes. He became the first Italian American to be nominated by either party in Illinois for a statewide office and he became the first Italian American to win a statewide election in Illinois history. The owner of Fast Freight was on a fast track.

As state treasurer, Cosentino championed the cause of the little guy, chastising banks for the usurious interest rates they charged on credit card debt. On the political front, he acted as Illinois chairman for President Carter's (unsuccessful) re-election race in 1980. His bid for the patronage-rich post of secretary of state in 1982 against Jim Edgar was a failure, but he bounced back and was elected for a second time as treasurer in 1986. In 1990, Cosentino again garnered the Democratic nomination for secretary of state against (ironically) George Ryan.

Cosentino seemed to be ahead in the race until charges surfaced of deceptive practices in his private trucking business. Though Cosentino was never accused of violating the public trust as an elected official, he lost the race for secretary of state, the traditional stepping stone to the governor's mansion, and his life went into a tailspin. He was convicted of some of the charges, sentenced to a fine and home confinement, and died in 1997 of complications related to diabetes.

For almost 20 years, Cosentino had been out there as a contender to be governor. His career embodied the highest political ambitions of Italian Americans in Illinois. Observers often refer to the Cosentino experience as the reason party leaders are reluctant to support Italian-named candidates. With Jerry Cosentino, Italian Americans finally got the break for which the ethnic group had been waiting a century, but were unable to capitalize on the opportunity.

On a less heady level in state government in the period from the 1970s to the 1990s, the original West Side Bloc was replaced by people who got better press. For instance State Representative Ralph Capparelli is the dean of the state house of representatives, currently serving his 33rd year in the Illinois House. Also in that group were more Republican suburbanites, like Aldo DeAngelis, not beholden to the Chicago Democratic machine. Downstaters like Edwardsville Democrat Sam Vadalabene (named Outstanding Legislator of 1969 by the Association of County Superintendents Schools), Rockford Democrat Zeke Giorgi (known as the father of the Illinois Lottery), Carlinville Representative Vince Demuzio (a onetime Democratic hopeful for secretary of state), and Spring Valley Democrat Richard Mautino (chair of the Small Business Committee), despite their party affiliation were equally free to practice a degree of independence and help combat the stereotypes.

For a few years in the 1990s sometime, State Representative Gary LaPaille chaired the state Democratic Party. Italian-American representation in the state legislature reached its peek in the 1993–1994 session when 16 of the 177 members of both houses were Italian—almost 10 percent representation from 5 percent of the population. This factoid gives credibility to the informed opinion of *Fra Noi* editor Paul Basile, who insists that recent Italian-American political leaders have been remarkably successful in light of the fact that the ethnic population is relatively small and scattered. Moreover, Italians seem to have been able to establish themselves in both parties, insuring access no matter who is in power.

DuPage County, west of Chicago, began booming in the post-war era, attracting many former city residents, including Italian Americans. Sheriff Richard Doria emerged in the 1970s and served at that post for over 20 years. In the late 1980s, a Republican Italian, Aldo Botti, was elected DuPage County Board President. This broke the mold. DuPage had only a small Italian population. The post was an executive one and the image of DuPage politics seems about as distant from the Old Machine as one could get.

This era also saw the appointment of several Italian-named men as assistants to Governor Walker (Victor De Grazia) in the 1970s and Governor Thompson (Henry Anselmo) in the 1980s. Exactly what impact these gentlemen had on policies or patronage affecting the Italian-American community is unclear. Walker's appointment of Anthony Sorrentino as director of the Commission on Delinquency Prevention was a recognition of Sorrentino's important role in the Italian-American community. Mayor Jane Byrne appointed an Italian American, Joe DiLeonardi, as the Chicago police chief in 1979. DiLeonardi went on to become a U.S. Marshal in Chicago, completing a 44-year career in law enforcement.

Republican Al Salvi became a major factor in statewide politics in the last half of the 1990s. A graduate of Notre Dame University and the University of Illinois Law School, Salvi served from 1992 to 1996 as a member of the Illinois House of Representatives from Lake County. His margin of victory in the 1994 election was 80–20 percent. He combined his ultra conservative politics with a clean cut image as the youthful father of six. Here was the opportunity of a lifetime to shatter the stereotypes, to make the kind of breakthrough for Italians in Illinois that John Kennedy had made for Catholics in 1960.

By running to the right in the 1996 Republican U.S. Senatorial primary, Salvi snagged the nomination from Lieutenant Governor Bob Kustra and won the right to go up against Dick Durbin. He lost badly in the general election. Salvi surfaced again in 1998 as the Republican candidate for Illinois Secretary of State, this time losing to Jesse White.

In 2002, Illinois got an Italian-American candidate for governor. The incumbent Republican Attorney General, Jim Ryan (who is Italian on his mother's side), ran unsuccessfully against Democrat Rod Blagojovich. Ryan's image was enhanced by the courageous way he and his family had coped with an overwhelming series of family medical problems. He was aided by a coterie of Justinian Society members who normally support the Democrats. However, in the absence of a compelling Italian-American candidate, it appears that Italian Americans with strong political convictions will vote party rather than ethnicity. Jim Ryan also had the disadvantage of having the same last name as the outgoing Governor George, who had been disgraced by a series of scandals dating back to his term as secretary of state.

A sampling of Italian-American participation in grassroots politics reveals heavy involvement. Historically, the number of Italians in the larger electoral units has never been great enough to successfully challenge other more populous ethnic groups. However, in electoral units such as suburbs like Chicago Heights, a base of 10,000 co-ethnics and a little coalition building can bring success, as it did for Mayor Charles Panici. Originally elected in 1975, Panici built up the most powerful Republican organization in the state, and his town was rewarded for that by a visit from President Reagan in 1986. Seven years later, Panici and most of his city council found themselves in federal prison convicted of bribery and racketeering.

On the plus side, a survey of the recent mayoral scene reveals that some key Italian-American mayors are leading their towns in a progressive direction. Anthony Vacco, the dean of Italian-American mayors, was for more than 30 years the mayor of Evergreen Park, a southwest adjacent suburb with a population of 21,000—mostly of Irish and Dutch descent and few Italians. A Republican turned Democrat, Vacco attributed his success to the respect that he showed toward all elements of his community, an attitude that he attributes to his Italian upbringing. Ron Serpico, the mayor of Melrose Park, sees himself as a reformer who also bases his political approach on respect. In 1995, he led an ethnic coalition that swept the long ensconced Italian-American incumbents from office. His ambition is to remold the image of Melrose Park by opening up the lines of communication within his community and by actively cooperating with neighboring municipalities.

In Chicago Heights, Democratic Mayor Angelo Ciambrone from 1995 to 2003 made great strides toward restoring the reputation of the town of 32,000 challenged by past political corruption and neglect. The author was a "participant observer" in Ciambrone's administration. Peter Silvestri creatively doubles as president of Elmwood Park and Cook County Commissioner. The suburbs of Burr Ridge and Frankfort also have had Italian-American mayors.

Italian-American aldermen, for example, have played influential roles in Blue Island. Rocco Guglielmucci and Michael Guglielmucci consecutively served from 1919 to 1941; Rocco Ziccardo, 1941–1960; John Rita, 1963–1978; Charley Esposito, 1966–1976; Rita was elected mayor of Blue Island for several terms in the 1970s and 1980s. Italian-named mayors are also a tradition in Highwood, Stone Park, and Elmwood Park.

In the mid-1990s Mayor Jerry Genova was doing such a good job of cleaning up Calumet City and ridding it of its "Sin Strip" that he has become the darling of the local press. Encouraged by this reception, Genova made a bid for state treasurer in the 1998 Democratic primary. Though unsuccessful, he seemed a likely candidate for higher office someday. All that speculation ended a few years later when he was indicted and convicted of diverting city resources and manpower for his personal gain. He served time in prison.

In 1994, a group of Italian Americans led by Anthony Tortoriello (an executive in the utility industry) formed the Italian American Political Coalition (IAPC). Although committees with similar names had surfaced in the past (usually during election years), the Italian American community never had a viable and continuing organization forthrightly devoted to the promotion of Italian-American interests in politics. The group aimed to provide a "political voice for the Italian American community" and it emphasized that the Italian vote could be the balance of power in any close election.

After considering all the foibles of such a venture, such as the diversity of class, politics, and geography within the Italian community, the IAPC settled on a formula. They would strive to register every Italian American in the state, to publicize political issues and candidates through statewide mailings, and, most importantly, to hold endorsement hearings to choose candidates most in tune with the Italian-American agenda. And high on that agenda was the recruitment and support of Italian-American candidates for as many offices as possible. The IAPC also appealed to the Italian-American public to break their long honored stereotype and contribute money to political causes like IAPC and the campaigns of individual Italian-American candidates. In short, the IAPC set up shop to become a credible player in the crowded arena of ethnic/interest group politics in Illinois.

The devil, however, is in the details. The IAPC's first major test came in the 1996 election when the lion's share of attention was focused on conservative State Senator Al Salvi's underdog bid to become U.S. Senator. With some notable exceptions, the IAPC was able to mobilize the Italian-American community behind Salvi with financial support and endorsements even from some lifelong liberal Democrats. The *Fra Noi* sang Salvi's praises and the IAPC did all the right things. The commitment to Salvi was greater than that given by the Italian-American public to any co-national in the history of Illinois. Unfortunately, Salvi was defeated 60 percent to 40 percent, rejected by the voters because of his conservative stances on abortion and gun control, and his own inept campaign tactics. In picking up the pieces after the wrecked campaign, some observers felt the IAPC had at least established its procedures that could be plugged in later to support a more viable candidate. Others more darkly suggested that the Salvi fiasco had proven once again how little the support of Italian Americans really matters.

Salvi managed to get on the Republican state ballot again in 1998, this time as a candidate for state treasurer. The IAPC under the leadership of its president, Anthony Fornelli (himself an aldermanic candidate a few years ago), went about IAPC business and endorsement efforts in the 1998 election without overemphasizing Salvi.

Meanwhile, the IAPC can look to a number of younger Italian political leaders who show some prospect of appealing to a broad enough spectrum of voters to get elected to higher office. Anyone of the following could possibly be the messiah who delivers Illinois Italians "Cuomo-like" from the agony and disrespect of being left out of the game. The aforementioned mayors or some of the Italian politicos who have emerged in DuPage county might be the ones. Alderman Charles Bernardini was originally appointed by Mayor Richard M. Daley to represent the upscale Lincoln Park area. Bernardini has an impressive resume as a top-level corporate attorney for Allstate Insurance, former Cook County Commissioner, and director of the American Chamber of Commerce in Italy. Chicago Democratic State Senator James De Leo worked very effectively to secure state grants for capital improvement of the Casa Italia campus. Richard Della Croce (who changed his name back from "Kress") is a former Village Trustee and former Democratic Township Committeeman in thriving (non-Italian) Orland Park.

Angelo "Skip" Saviano went from a position of supervisor of Leyden Township to Republican state representative from the Melrose Park area. Mentored by Senator DeAngelis, Saviano is encouraged by the de facto Italian-American caucus in the state legislature to preserve Columbus Day as a national holiday. Second generation State Representative Frank Mautino from the Spring Valley area has shown considerable interest in education issues. Another young, personable leader, Cook County Commissioner and mayor of Elmwood Park, Peter Silvestri, seems eminently capable of expanding his political base far beyond his West Suburban district. And Debbie DeFrancesco Halvorson, who toppled DeAngelis in the South Suburbs, might very well be a viable candidate for a future statewide ticket.

One of the most effective political forces in promoting an Italian-American agenda has been Italian Consul General Granara who marshalled support from the Sons of Italy, the National Italian American Foundation (NIAF), and Italian-American legislators in Springfield to secure funding for the expansion of Italian language instruction in public schools.

After more than a century of venal efforts, false starts, missed opportunities, and small successes, Italian-American political leaders stand at the brink of an uncertain future. No one knows quite what the meaning and purpose of Italian or any other kind of ethnicity will be in the twenty-first century. But it is clear that those with higher ambitions need to broaden their base, become inter-ethnic diplomats, perhaps to fashion a coalition of elements who share traditional cultural values and common economic interests. The presence of Italian Americans in the councils of both parties is an encouraging sign. And despite all the imperfections of Chicago and Illinois politics, the one certainty that reins is that the bad old days of gangster-ridden and machine dominated politics are all but gone.

Chapter Six

CHICAGO'S ITALIANS IN LABOR UNIONS AND BUSINESSES

Italian immigrants came to America for *pane e lavoro*. In the multi-generational process of securing for themselves and their families the bread and work that was their original object, they also accumulated some *potere*, power derived from their organization in the work place and their position in the world of commerce.

In the early years of Italian immigration, there was a class struggle going on throughout the country. Immigration policy was liberal exactly because industrial leaders feared that a labor shortage would drive up wages and drive down industrial profits. Most industries skillfully played their workers from different national backgrounds against each other to avoid unions. If the workers couldn't communicate with each other because of language problems, so much the better. Government almost invariably supported big business against labor. By today's standards, workers were oppressed and the legal system denied them the basic right to organize. Chicago had seen labor violence in the Haymarket Riot of 1886, the Pullman Strike in 1894, and in a host of smaller labor disputes. The struggle between labor and capital created a dangerous and unscrupulous environment. But slowly, in the first decade of the twentieth century, workers began to make progress.

The socialists made a strong bid to organize Italian immigrants in Chicago. In the eastern part of the country, Italians had joined and organized garment workers', stone workers', and building industry trade unions before 1900. On the other hand, after the turn of the century, Italians gained a reputation in some instances as strikebreakers. They crossed the lines in a cigar strike and in a luggage workers' strike. Italian radicals and unionists had their work cut out for them. As Miller and Panofsky have written:

> The militant radicals placed themselves, in a sense, at the opposite end of the Italian cultural spectrum. Theirs was a world of relative values, entirely immersed in history and politics, unlike the apolitical, eternal world of the contadini. The response of the *contadini* to their tragic and static conception of existence was one of heroic self-denial

> and ingenuity. Their endurance and patience tapped the opportunities offered by the new economic system, resulting at times in modest family accumulation. . . . Fundamental to their [the socialists] thinking was a profound faith in the inevitable triumph of their struggle. . . . The "*pensier ribelle*" [rebellious mode of thinking] and an identification with the international proletariat filtered their perception of the world and generated a strong revulsion against established religion, the clergy, superstition, and patriotism. . . . Their political activities, work experience, and social lives blended into one. Their spare time was given over to meetings, organizing and cultural activities, to be shared by family members. Recreation was not only of educational importance but a tactical and even an economic tool: Picnics, raffles, plays, music, lectures, public debates and rallies which filled holidays and weekends built a social bond and so became also a part of the proselytizing function.

Giuseppe Bertelli (1870–1943) was the acknowledged leader of the Italian socialist movement in Chicago for almost 40 years. He was born in Florence. Prior to coming to Chicago, Bertelli spent 15 years as a social activist in Italy first as editor of *Il Pioniere* (the Pioneer), a socialist youth publication, and then as editor of Trieste's weekly socialist newspaper, *Il Lavoratore*. Because the Italian government considered him subversive, Bertelli's migration to Chicago in June 1906 was more a push from Italy rather than a pull toward Chicago.

Bertelli hit the ground running, establishing *La Parola dei Socialisti* as the voice of the Italian Socialist Federation in Chicago. Bertelli was very actively involved in the garment strikes between 1910 and 1920 as a speaker and his newspaper acted as a cheerleader and guide for Italian workers venturing into the class struggle. When Woodrow Wilson declared war in 1917, *La Parola dei Socialisti* was in the forefront of the opposition to the "capitalist" war. So objectionable did the federal government find *La Parola*'s criticism that the paper was banned from the federal mail. To get around this restriction, the editors simply changed the name of the publication to *La Parola del Proletario*. When postal authorities discovered this subterfuge, the name became *La Parola del Popolo*. Eventually, the post office threatened heavy fines, and the socialists resorted to shipping the subversive paper in boxes identified as "canned tomatoes," "spaghetti," or "medicine." The packages were directed to friends who would distribute them by hand to the people.

In 1926, Egidio Clemente appeared on the socialist scene in Chicago. On and off for the next five decades Clemente carried the torch for socialism in Chicago as the editor of *La Parola del Popolo*. He interrupted his task only during World War II, when he joined the OSS to aid the propaganda effort to overthrow Mussolini. His full-length interview on this subject appears in *Voices Of America: Italians in Chicago*.

While the socialist revolution never came, change did occur. Nelli, points out that between 1900 and 1920, Italians in Chicago played major roles in joining and organizing the following unions: the sewer and tunnel workers, the hod carriers, the macaroni makers, garment workers, mosaic workers, pressmen, cigar makers, barbers, bakers, and bricklayers. And they were present as members in "American" unions that included masons, carpenters, and typographical workers.

Chicago Italians were early to dominate one major union and they continued to reign over it for the rest of the century. The Hod Carriers' Union first organized in 1903 and was affiliated with the American Federation of Labor. Many of this union's early publications were in Italian and most of the delegates to its 1911 national meeting were Italian immigrants. Also in that period in Chicago, D'Andrea directed field work among Italian workers to create more locals in Chicago for the hod carriers. The busy D'Andrea simultaneously served as business agent for the sewer and tunnel workers. In 1910 while he was a candidate for the state senate, his criminal past caught up with him and he was defeated. Though he died a few years later, the victim of murder, D'Andrea's efforts gave a voice to the workers and an important role for Chicago Italians in the future of the union.

In 1926, Joseph Moreschi, a Chicago Italian, was elected international president. He served until 1967 and was succeeded by fellow Chicagoans Peter and Angelo Fosco. While the above accomplishments of the Foscos certainly were of great benefit to their family, the question arises as to how this impacted the *paesano* on the street. The testimony of immigrants from Pizzone, a small Molisano town a few miles from Castel di Sangro (Abruzzi), gives us a glimpse into the dynamic of how the success of the Foscos in the Laborers' Union benefited the larger group.

Pizzonese immigrants to Chicago were aided and encouraged by access to the Hod Carriers' Union (later referred to as the Laborers' International Union of North America or LIUNA). Born of Pizzonesi parents in Russia in 1894, Fosco emigrated to Chicago in 1913. In 1915, he became the business agent for the Hod Carriers' Union. It seems logical that the large number of Chicago Italians, especially Abruzzese, in the ranks of unskilled construction laborers, contributed to Fosco's early success as did his relationship by marriage to hod carrier and sewer tunnel union leaders Joseph and Anthony D'Andrea. Fosco became a citizen in 1918. In that same year he became president of Local Number 2 of the Laborers' Union, an office he held until 1936 when he became regional head of the national union.

In his role as politician, Peter Fosco was the Democratic Committeeman from the first ward from 1938 to 1951 and served as a Cook County Commissioner from 1938 to 1944. He became president of the 600,000-member International Laborers' Union in 1967, succeeding Moreschi. Peter Fosco served until his death in 1975 and was succeeded in the presidency of the union by his son, Angelo. Though dogged by allegations of corruption, Angelo Fosco continued to preside over what is probably the most Italian of North America's large labor unions, collecting a salary in 1986 of $146,000. He served as president until he was removed by federal authorities in the 1990s. Though the national and local leadership of LIUNA often handled business affairs in a scandalous manner, damage to individual members was limited. On a basic level, the Laborers' Union got the job done by improving wages and working conditions and providing pensions.

As detailed in Peter Pero's 1978 article in *La Parola del Popolo* "A Brief History of Italians in Chicago's Labor Movement," Italians were also the prime movers in the formation of the Amalgamated Clothing Workers Union, which grew out of the 1910 Chicago strike against Hart, Schaffner, and Marx. Tradition has it that the strike began on September 29 when a humble Sicilian seamstress, disgusted with the abuses of the shop foremen, led 3,000 workers out on strike. Soon over 20,000 were out on strike.

Though the basic issues were not resolved, the strike did result in the founding of the Amalgamated Clothing Workers Union of America under the leadership of Chicagoans Anzuino D. Marimpietri and Emilio Grandinetti.

When Anzuino Marimpietri (1881–1975) came to America as teenager, he was already a skilled tailor and soon went to work in the Chicago clothing industry. He attended night school classes and took correspondence courses to improve his education. When the strike started he was working at Hart, Shaffner, and Marx, and when the strike ended after 17 weeks of struggle, he was a recognized union leader. Because the garment workers in 1910 were almost all new immigrants, they did not speak each other's language or English very well. In addition, the issues of those who worked on diverse parts of productions varied. This sometimes meant that strike rallies and deliberations had to be divided both by language and work specialty. In fact, it often took 16 separate halls to accommodate simultaneous meetings of the diverse groups involved in the strike. Conflicts with the police and other adversities effectively radicalized the workers and created the unity necessary for launching the ACWA. Future ACWA leaders like Clara Masilotti and Andrea Marotta also emerged from the struggle.

By 1919, virtually all the clothing workers in Chicago were unionized. Italian locals, especially Chapter 270, under the leadership of Louis Chiostra (a native of Ponte Buggianese, Lucca), were in the forefront of the ACWA movement. As described by Peter Pero, the ACWA organized in 1922 one of the first labor-owned banks in the nation, the Amalgamated Trust and Savings, and Marimpietri was one of its vice-presidents.

Grandinetti was born in Catanzaro in 1882 and studied to be an engineer. He joined the socialist movement of the period and wrote articles attacking the King. Under threat of a jail sentence, he emigrated to the United States in 1908. Soon he found himself in Chicago, working with Bertelli and writing for *La Parola dei Socialiasti*. When the 1910 strike began, Grandinetti was enlisted as a speaker, and his eloquence convinced the Italian workers to stay the course. His success led him to a lifelong career as an organizer for ACWA as it moved from a socialist position toward the mainstream liberal Democratic philosophy.

The success of the Amalgamated was a perfect fit. The Italian tradition of tailoring had prepared vast numbers of both men and women to be productive workers in the increasingly centralized garment industry. The ejection of many radical subversives from Italy gave the Chicago group some able leaders to work within and through the vigorous socialist movement in the city. The unceasing efforts of the socialists to teach, inform, and propagandize ultimately reached the workers on the shop floor. And it is they, with their individual and group decisions to strike, who willed this union into existence. The ACWA's business affairs have been apparently well managed.

After 1920, Chicago Italian Americans increased the pace over which they acquired power in organized labor and they often did it in fields related to Italian cultural or occupational traditions. In the field of music, James "Caesar" Petrillo (1892–1984) emerged in the 1920s on the Chicago scene. Petrillo, the son of a sewer digger, grew up on DeKoven on the Near West Side. He attended programs at Hull House where, it is said, he learned to play the trumpet and was a member of the Boys Band. He quit school after completing only the fourth grade to start a dance band with three of his friends, and they became members of the Chicago Federation of Musicians Local 10. Wags have maintained that he got into union organizing because his talents as a musician were meager.

No one could doubt Petrillo's organizing talents. In 1920, he was elected vice president of the Chicago Union and in 1923, president. In 1940, Petrillo was elected president of the American Federation of Musicians Union (national), a position he held until 1958. After he stepped down from that position, he moved back to Chicago as president of Local 10. Local 10 was all white and Local 208 represented African-American musicians. Petrillo had always resisted merging the two unions and it was on this issue that insurgents were able to unseat him in 1962. Ironically, Petrillo bounced back in 1964, arranging for the national union to appoint him chair of its civil rights commission. It is reported that he toured the country for the next few years and actually was quite effective in his mission.

Petrillo was tough. He protested to Chicago politicians and even to Mussolini when events that they sponsored failed to use union musicians. Before 1920, the only way to hear music was to be in the presence of live musicians or play a scratchy Victrola. Then new technology brought big challenges. Petrillo led his union through some difficult times as 78 r.p.m. records, radio and the "talkies," and television and networks transformed the entertainment industry, threatening the very livelihood of musicians (and their union). During the Depression, he allocated union funds to stage free public concerts in Grant Park in order to create work for his union musicians. City fathers have kept up the tradition and today the bandshell in Grant Park bears his name.

Because he was so tough and because his actions had dramatic impact on the high profile entertainment business, Petrillo's name became a household word. A major breakthrough was his 1930s contract with WMAQ in which the radio station guaranteed the jobs of its "studio orchestra." His campaign against "canned music" and the strike actions he took against big networks like NBC and the Boston Symphony drew a lot of criticism from the public. During World War II he banned union musicians from making recordings for a period in 1942 until the record industry would agree to his demand to create a Music Performance Trust Fund (derived from record sales) to pay musicians to give free concerts. Twice Petrillo's image graced the cover of *Time* Magazine. He has earned a place in the history of Italian Americans because of his feisty defense of his interest group—the musicians— a sizable number of whom were Italian Americans.

Of the many anecdotes about him, Anthony Scariano's account of the "Petrillo Handshake" is the most bizarre. Apparently suffering from a germ phobia, Petrillo would shake hands only by extending his "pinky" finger.

In the period before 1935, the labor movement had an image of idealistic radical social reform. As we have seen, socialists and even communists mixed freely and seemed to cooperate during strikes. Before the Communist Revolution in Russia in 1917, American socialism had a degree of respectability. But when the Russian communists declared their intention to spread their socialist revolution to every corner of the globe, the reaction in America was the Red Scare. After that event, conventional wisdom defined socialism as outright subversive and traitorous. In a sense, it became more acceptable to American public opinion for the labor movement to be infiltrated by gangsters than by socialists. The case of the Italian Bread Drivers' strike and the murder of Giovanni Pippan (1894–1933) apparently was a turning point in this process.

Pippan was born in Trieste and gained a reputation as a brilliant organizer of miners in the coal fields off the Adriatic coast. He was an officer in the Socialist Party of the city of Albona. This brought him into conflict with armed fascist groups who made it so uncomfortable for him and his family that they fled to the United States, where he was well received by Italian Socialists throughout the nation. He became a member of the American Communist Party from 1926 to 1931. In that year he returned to Chicago where he was asked to help the Italian bread drivers. They were seeking recognition of their union and higher wages. Reportedly, Pippan was able to negotiate an agreement, except for one issue: the bread stamp. The Bakery Owners Association wanted the drivers to make sure that every loaf they delivered had a stamp on it and that every stamp was paid for.

The major bakeries in Chicago had formed an owners' association, which ostensibly was supported by a 1¢ stamp affixed to each delivered loaf of bread. A penny was added to the price of each loaf bearing the stamp. It is unclear where the revenues from these stamps was supposed to be going, but everyone knew that it was for "protection." Egidio Clemente and others close to Pippan advised him to accept the deal, since the bread drivers got everything they wanted. Pippan, however, was shocked and offended by the request to do the bidding of racketeers and held his ground, and ostensibly he got his way. But 90 days after a victory celebration attended by union members and the bakery owners, Pippan was shot dead in broad daylight on August 29, 1933, as he walked to a streetcar stop in Cicero. Though two men were arrested fleeing the scene, there were no convictions. Most observers took this murder to be symbolic of the victory of the organized crime element in the Italian-American labor movement over the socialist idealist element.

Unskilled workers in steel mills gained union recognition in the late 1930s and during World War II. From the mid-1930s, the struggle to organize all ranks of the steel workers into one big industrial union was intense. Two of the ten worker killed by authorities in the 1937 Memorial Day Massacre at Republic Steel on the South Side, Anthony Tagliori and Leo Francisco, were among the strikers trying to set up a picket line when they were struck down. Reaction to this event marked a turning point in the effort to establish industrial unions of unskilled workers in the steel industry and the dead have been honored as martyrs to the cause of organized labor.

For over 30 years Joe Germano served as director of the United Steel Workers' Association (USWA) district, which included northeastern Illinois and northern Indiana. Another protégé of the Steel Workers in this era was Frank Annunzio, who was in charge of education and legislative affairs for the USWA. Raymond Sarocco and Joe LaMorte organized many locals of the union around South Chicago, Harvey, and Chicago Heights. According to historian Peter Pero, other Italian-American point men for the USWA were Nicholas Fontecchio, Carl Alessi, Joseph Cesario, Paul Markonni, John Alesia, and James Pinta. The successful organization of the steel workers, the wage hikes, and benefits that accrued brought a measure of security and prosperity to hundreds of Italian-American steel worker families in Chicago Heights and Melrose Park.

Undoubtedly the same can be said for Italian-American workers from 24th and Oakley, who toiled at the International Harvester Plant (McCormick Reaper Works) at Western and Blue Island. Tony Cavorso evolved as a union worker and Pete Neputi was president of McCormick Local Union. Tony Audia was a union veteran who helped organize Chicago's first chapter of the United Auto Workers in 1938. He went on to negotiate nearly 2,500 contract settlements.

Ernest Demaio was a founding member since 1936 of the United Electrical Workers Union. He was active in Chicago as an anti-fascist in the 1930s and during World War II as a member of the Italian American Victory Council. Demaio eventually got involved in the worldwide labor movement through the United Nations.

One of the most effective and yet one of the most notorious unions in the nation is the Teamsters' Union. Chicago Italians have played a prominent role on both the local and national level. Daniel Collucio organized the tobacco and confectionery vending machine workers Local 761; Michael Formusa was a civil rights activist within the Teamsters organization; Ray Domenic organized farm workers in the area; in the 1970s, James E. Coli controlled the funeral industry Local 727; Domenic Senese served as the secretary-treasurer of the Produce and Dairy Haulers Local 703.

Especially controversial was Joseph Glimco Sr., the head of the Teamster Cab Drivers' Local 777. Accused of strong-arm tactics in a 1950s cab drivers' strike, Glimco was a good friend of Jimmy Hoffa and was reportedly one of those responsible for the strong support that Chicago Teamsters gave to Hoffa in his successful bid to become the the president of the International Brotherhood of the Teamsters.

While condemning corrupt unions, some Italian-American observers note that various federal government task forces have been very aggressive in rooting out corruption among Teamster and Laborers' Union officials and somewhat less aggressive when going after white collar criminals in big business. So-called "Strike Forces" have made great progress in the last few decades and they may indeed have brought organized crime in Chicago under control. In any case, a sharp decline in the number of Italian-named corrupt union leaders is a welcome development.

Though the information we have is sketchy, Italians were apparently active in a wide range of other activities promoting organized labor in job classifications traditionally held by Italians. Vito Losito helped to organize shoe workers, to get raises for counter clerks, and to get more generous work rules for shoe shine boys. Patsy Trotta, Tony Adduci, Frank D'Rango, and Tom Siracusa from 1900 did organizational work among Italian barbers. The barbers union was successful at standardizing service and preventing cut-throat competition. Siracusa served for several decades as president of the group.

Paul Iaccino worked as director of the AFL-CIO community services department. He also helped create the Chicago branch of the Italian American Labor Council (IALC) in 1966. Joseph Sippa and Henry Coco headed up the Printing Trades Council, one of the oldest trade unions in the city. Coco also lobbied successfully for the law that prohibits the importation of professional strike breakers in Illinois. Peter Carbonara served in the 1920s as president of the bakery union and worked to prevent racketeering and corruption in the union. Hotel and restaurant service employees in Chicago were represented by Fred Albi, who organized the Sherman House, Morrison, Harrison, Midland, Continental Plaza, and Palmer House Hotels. Fred Rizzo was for a time the union representative for the dining room employees, cooks, and bartenders union. Carl Sanzone and Joseph Ungari are remembered for their pioneer organizing of the retail and wholesale trades. Ungari personally organized unions at Sears, Polk Brothers, National Foods, Community Discount, Robert Hall, and Montgomery Ward stores. Elia Mosesso, an immigrant from Abruzzi, helped organize retail clerks. Joe Giganti worked to create a college teachers union.

The Italian American Labor Council was established in 1966 to increase communication among Italian Americans across a variety of industries and to preserve the heritage of labor activism among Chicago's Italians. The council also worked to help newly-arrived immigrants from Italy, to encourage Italian Americans to join unions, and to combat defamatory attacks on Italian Americans. Like other Italian-American organizations, the IALC had as its goal full representation of Italian Americans in the political and social scheme in Chicago on par with the size of the Italian-American population.

According to its longtime president Joe Rovai, the IALC was similar to other ethnic and racial groups who have formed organizations to advance their particular interests. At first Rovai ran into opposition because some felt ethnic identity was a thing of the past, that the melting pot had done its work. "We had all come here, we had done well. There was no discrimination as far as individuals attaining their positions. [But] as time went on the membership increased to 600 because Italian Americans saw other minorities attain the benefits of ethnic organization."

Over the twentieth century, it seems clear that organized labor has advanced the fortunes of Italian Americans as individuals and as a group. They benefited directly as participants in unions like the laborers', clothing workers', and musicians' unions that included a lot of Italians, and they benefited from the success of the AFL-CIO general campaign for better wages and benefits for all workers. Of course, individual Italian-American labor leaders gained wealth and power from the movement. Some of them had unsavory ties. Though it was an imperfect passage from *braccianti* to *signori* (with a union card) marked by setbacks and even betrayals, Chicago's Italians were served well by the broader union movement—so well, that poverty is virtually unknown among the Italians in Chicago.

Italians have been in business in Chicago since the 1850s. And while the immigrant stereotype of the poor, illiterate, and unskilled laborer is essentially true, it is also true that prosperous business families have been a unique factor in the Italian immigrant experience in Chicago from the very beginning. Playing from their strong suit, Italian enterprise focused on food. The Dominick's Grocery slogan, "People who really know their food!" captures the essence of Italian entrepreneurship in Chicago. Whether it was the importation of olive oil or wine for fellow Italians or the importation of produce from Termini Imerese in Sicily, the New Orleans market, or California for the general market, Italian entrepreneurs, big and small, were there. Macaroni factories, mom and pop groceries, fish stores, and butchershops fueled Italian businesses in Chicago from the 1880s.

Italian businesses in Chicago were family businesses, handed down from one generation to the next. And though the company names usually included only males, the wives and daughters of those "father-and-son" businesses were just as likely to be responsible for the success of the business.

This segment of the narrative just scratches the surface of the 150-year process by which Italians integrated into the world of business in Chicago and the Midwest. This random sampling of business personalities and trends provides strong evidence of the entrepreneurial skills and work ethnic that helped move Italian Americans up the ladder of social mobility in Chicago. A full treatment of the subject, on the scale of the study by Miller and Panofsky on Italian socialists, should be done.

In an article entitled "Our Italian Brethren," the *Tribune* on Sunday, April 11, 1886, stated that "Italian immigration is far from being an unmitigated evil that some people seem to think." The article went on to point out that the northern Italians were "progressive citizens, become Americanized rapidly, and contribute a fair share to the Nation." The Genoese were described as "natural fruit handlers" and the article claimed that Garibaldi and Cuneo, A.J. Arata, Solcese and Lagorio, Angelo Matteo, and Raggio and John Borizzolara had a virtual monopoly on fruit selling in the South Water Market. Moreover, the reporter claimed that there were over a dozen Chicago Italians worth more that $250,000 in cash or improved property.

In 1907, John F. Cuneo, a descendant of the founding Genovese families, at the age of 21 bought up the bankrupt Jenkins & George bookbinding business, and changed its name to John F. Cuneo Company. Business was good. At the end of World War I Cuneo took over the Henneberry Company, a major printing and book-making business. And in 1924 he bought the giant Sears printing plant. These assets in the mid-1920s were the foundation for the Cuneo Printing Corporation empire that eventually included vast printing facilities in Chicago, New York, and Philadelphia. The Cuneo family is a major philanthropist in the Chicago area and has given large gifts to Cabrini hospital and the Loyola University Medical Center. Frank Cuneo in 1910 was a prominent real estate developer who built a block of stores that formed the heart of the Wilson Avenue business district at Sheridan Road.

Another early success story was Gaetano D'Amico, who arrived in the United States in 1889 from Abruzzi. After working on the railroad in Missouri, he moved to Chicago in 1892, then to Chicago Heights in 1895. Seven years later, his family opened up a grocery store in the heart of the 22nd Street commercial district, while he continued to work at Inland Steel. The success of this business brought capital, which the family invested in a macaroni business at 17th and Lowe. "Mamma Mia" brand spaghetti products, bearing the picture of D'Amico's wife, Giacinta, sold well, and the company expanded into a larger factory in Steger.

With the support of the Italian Consul General, Guido Sabetti, and the leadership of the Cuneo family, Italian-American businesses came together in 1907 to form the Italian American Chamber of Commerce of Chicago (IACC). While oriented toward import-export commerce with Italy, the IACC created a commercial fraternity where some 260 Italians in all fields of businesses could network and exchange their goods and services.

On October 6, 1907, the Italian chargé d'affaires Montagna accepted the charter of the Chicago IACC. The first president of IACC was Frank Cuneo (of Garibaldi and Cuneo). Graciano Allegretti, Pietro Costa, Giuilo Piazza, and Modestino Mastro-Giovanni were the officers. Notable names among the board of directors were Andrea Cuneo, Alessandro Mastro-Valerio, Giovanni Garibaldi, and Bernard Barasa. Though Italian-American entrepreneurship and business success ranged well beyond the IACC, the membership continued to be among the Italians most identified with their cultural heritage. The activities of a few of the early members of the IACC provide us with a snapshot of Italians in Chicago commerce.

Louis Caravetta (1879–1945) from Consenza worked his way up from Longhi Imports, Cihral Cheese (which he renamed Caravetta) by developing markets among the Italian miners in Illinois, Indiana, Minnesota, Michigan, Colorado, and Montana. Caravetta's main warehouse was at 33–35 West Kinzie in a distinctive brick building accented by white limestone. Like most other businesses of the time, it was family based and passed on to Caravetta's sons upon his death. He was president of the IACC during World War II. Caravetta's management skills were such that the Chicago Italian Chamber of Commerce was the only Italian chamber in the country to continue (limited) operations. This, despite the fact that federal agents confiscated all of its records and office machines following the declaration of war in 1941.

Other notables include Vincenzo Formusa, who began a company with his family name in 1898 for the importation of macaroni and olive oil from his home town of Termini Imerese in Sicily. Like other successful Italian food importers, Formusa looked to the whole Midwest region as his market. The business passed on to his sons Pietro and Giuseppe, who weathered the interruption of trade caused by World War II.

Carlo Ginnocchio from Burzonsca (Genoa, 1852) came to Chicago in the 1870s and worked his way up in the wine business and eventually formed his own wine import business. As the Chamber *Bulletin* put it "he prospered in a way that ensured his family notable comfort" (author's translation). He was perhaps the most popular Italian personality in Chicago, a member and officer of many Italian clubs. He used his influence as president of the Garibaldi Society to induce the Italian colony and the city fathers to cooperate in the erection of a monument to the "Hero of two continents" in Lincoln Park.

Frank Muzzuchelli was president and Antonio Mattucci treasurer of Milano Furniture on West 47th Street. Andrea Russo (1859–1935) was born in San Concardio (Lucca) and in 1885 founded a macaroni importing and manufacturing concern on Chicago Avenue. He, of course, passed on the family business to his sons, Andrea and Charles.

In 1886 in a basement shop on DeKoven Street, Alessandro Gonnella produced a few hundred loaves of bread for sale from his small storefront bakery on the Near West Side. A decade later with the help of his wife, Marianna Marcucci of Barga (Lucca), Gonnella moved operations to Sangamon and Ohio Streets. Chain migration brought his brothers-in-law, who found ready employment at the bakery that sent out fleets of horse-drawn wagons to deliver the bread to thousands of homes, grocery stores, and restaurants. To this day, some 33 members of the Gonnella-Marcucci families continue the business, producing over a million pounds of bread each week.

In 1933, there were more than 180 members in the chamber that included John F. Cuneo and his giant printing business; Lorenzo Marcucci, manager of Gonnella bakery; the Rago Brothers Funeral Home near Grand and Western; a sprinkling of pharmacists, grocers, doctors, lawyers, and one politician (State Representative Michael Pluro). The largest category of membership was in the wholesale food business; 12 were in the olive oil business alone. Clearly, the foodways of Italy and the talents of Lucchese, Genoese, and Sicilian entrepreneurs paved the way for fast track success for a significant portion of Italians in Chicago. Since the IACC was oriented toward the international trade, there are only a few building contractors or restaurateurs on the early membership lists.

Some factoids that emerge from a random perusal of the Chicago Italian American Chamber of Commerce *Bulletin* from 1907 to 1950 are: the first mention of pizza is in 1943—Paterno's Pizzeria (Grand and Western); the first mention of Italian movies in Chicago came in 1948, *Furia*, starring Rossano Brazzi and Isa Pola at the Annex (3200 W. Madison); Bragno and Company Wines and Liquors were an advertising mainstay in the *Bulletin*; Domenico Cambio of Conte di Savoia (1012 S. Halsted) was a perennial winner of the chamber's window decorating contests; there was an abrupt language switch from mostly Italian before World War II to mostly English during and after the war.

A regular advertiser in the *Bulletin*, The Daprato Statuary Company, urged readers to "Keep Your Church Beautiful with Daprato Productions" and listed their locations as Chicago, New York, and Pietrasanta (Italy). Since many of its members had been wine importers, the chamber welcomed the end of Prohibition in 1933 with a cartoon that depicted "Legal Beer" as the prodigal son returning to father "Common Sense."

Chicago Italian Americans on the business horizon today continue to engage in the traditional commerce of food. Highest profile is the Dominick's Grocery chain, started by Dominick Di Matteo in 1918 in a 20 by 50 foot storefront at 3842 W. Ohio Street. Though they didn't add another store until 1934, over three generations the chain grew to almost 100 stores. Its reputation for exacting Italian quality standards was used in marketing the Dominick's staff as "people who really know their food."

Though Dominick's merged into the Safeway system, the name remains. In the course of its remarkable growth, Mr. "D" and Dominick Jr. offered employment in the 1950s to many Italian Americans whose corner stores were being knocked out of business by the trend toward large supermarkets.

Candy played a role in the lives of many Italian Americans. Chicago was for a long time the Candy Capital of the country. Women worked at Brach's and other candy factories located north and west of the Loop. One enterprising immigrant, Salvatore Ferrara, brought with him in 1900 the skills he had learned in Nola (Campania) for making sugar coated almonds, the "confetti." An essential part of Italian weddings, they are a symbol of fertility. Ferrara first took a job on the Santa Fe Railroad as an interpreter between the bosses and the Italian *braccianti*. In 1908, he settled in Chicago to establish a candy-pastry shop that grew into a larger candy factory at 2200 W. Taylor, the site of the original Ferrara Bakery.

Mariano Turano came to Chicago from Castrolibero, Calabria, in 1955 to join his brother Carmen, a baker and grocer who had emigrated in 1922. Mariano worked on construction and helped out in the bakery. After bringing his whole family to Chicago, Mariano in 1962 bought a bakery of his own, the Campagna Bakery, on the Northwest Side. In 1966, Mariano, Carmen, and a third brother, Eugene, established the Campagna-Turano Bakery at 6441 W. Roosevelt in Berwyn.

They built up a clientele with their famous four-pound loaf. Mariano's boys, Renato, Tony, and Giancarlo, grew up in the business—making home deliveries, cleaning up, and baking bread. Forty years later, Turano has become a regional giant with three large plants, a sophisticated distribution system to their regional market, and a joint venture agreement with Sara Lee. The three boys are still working together, having created an industry out of their father's bakery. In the tradition of Chicago's Italian-American food-related businesses, the Turanos are preparing for the third generation to enter the business. The Turanos are also deeply involved in the Italian-American community, especially the Casa Italia.

Anthony Paterno migrated to the United States from Vizzini (near Catania) to the Grand and Western area. He emerged as an active member of the IACC in the late 1940s when he ran a liquor store, grocery store, and small restaurant pizzeria. He grew these enterprises into Paterno Imports (1964) and Pacific Wine with the help of talented nephews imported from Sicily (Dominick and John Buffalino) and recruited his son-in-law Anthony Terlato. After the death of Paterno in the early 1980s, Terlato took control and built an even bigger empire based on his discovery of Santa Margherita Pinot Grigio.

While Paterno was enormously active in the Italian community, serving as president of the IACC (1952–1954), the JCCIA (1963–1964), and the Italo American National Union, Terlato was focused entirely on the business, which now includes ownership of four California wineries, joint ventures in France and Australia, ownership of Tangley Oaks (the former Armour Mansion), and a sales force of over 120.

The stellar rise of Jerry Colangelo is an example of how the success of an outstanding individual can impact the group. Colangelo grew up on the Hill in Chicago Heights and starred in baseball and basketball at Bloom High School. He made the All–Big Ten Basketball Team in his senior year at the University of

Illinois. In the mid-1960s he got a job in management with Jerry Kraus and the fledgling Chicago Bulls. A few years later he worked his way up to become the general manager of the Phoenix Suns, then owner of the baseball Diamondbacks, and in 2001 the owner of the winner of the World Series. Though no longer a Chicagoan, one of Jerry's many charities is the Italian American Sports Hall of Fame (IASHF). Many credit Colangelo with raising the funds to finance the IASHF's new building on Taylor Street.

Pasquale Caputo (Mola di Bari) and his wife Rene started off in 1978 running a cheese store, then moved into the cheese production business promoting themselves at Feste Italiana and supplying grated mozzarella to pizzerias. Over the next two decades, Pasquale and Rene saw the family business grow into WISCON Cheese Corporation with 80 employees. In the 1990s, he bought the Olimpio Milan Basketball Team and later sold a 50 percent share to Kobe Bryant of the Los Angeles Lakers. For several whirlwind years he created sports exchanges and even a youth basketball camp at Casa Italia in Stone Park. The basketball adventure proved shortlived and Caputo soon sold off his interest, satisfied that he had saved the team and enriched the future of professional basketball in Italy.

In 1995, the *Fra Noi* Directory accumulated a definitive list of Italian-American organizations and businesses in the Chicago area. There are over 1,000 Italian restaurants, 63 bakeries, 41 banquet halls, 47 caterers, and 116 grocery stores in the Chicago area. More than half of these operations appear to be family businesses. The current advertising in the *Fra Noi* and various dinner-dance ad books reflects a slightly broader spectrum for Italian-American enterprise. Though the food-related products and services still dominate, legal, dental, and medical professionals, real estate agents, funeral directors, travel agencies, banks, and jewelers also advertise.

Of course success in business has made a better life for the business people and their families. It has provided role models to others in the ethnic group. In a small business environment, the jobs created by successful businesses often went to Italians in the neighborhood. Successful businessmen (and women) with a "habit of command" can often transfer that trait to community leadership. And Italian-American businessmen have enhanced the quality of life for Italians and all Chicagoans by providing their food products to a city hungry for Italian delicacies.

Most Italian business people have given at least a portion of their charitable contributions to Italian community projects such as the Villa Scalabrini. The community benefits when they compete with each other for the honor of being considered the most generous. More often, business leaders have allowed themselves to be feted at "men of the year" dinners, for which their friends and business associates are solicited for fundraiser tickets and ad book tributes. Most surprising was a gift from Mary Ellen Mancina Batinich and Alex Batinich of $250,000 to support the Immigration History Research Center at the University of Minnesota.

Others who have accumulated fortunes have guided their philanthropy to mainstream and high-visibility medical or educational causes. The Cuneo gifts to the Cabrini Hospital and the Loyola Medical School and Dino D'Angelo's $10 million gift to the University of Chicago Law School are but two examples. Automobile dealer Joe Gentile has made a number of high profile gifts to Loyola University, St. Ignatius High School, and Our Lady of Pompeii Shrine.

Chapter Seven

ITALIAN OR AMERICAN? WORLD WAR II CHANGED EVERYTHING

The 1930s and 1940s created an identity crisis for Italians in America. On the one hand, the near-universal admiration for Mussolini in the 1920s and early 1930s pulled Italians to identify with the Old Country. On the street, in the churches and schools, and in the workplace most people continued to identify themselves and each other with reference to their European country of origin. Even in the second generation few would have identified themselves as "Americans." The outbreak of World War II cleared the air. The first generation woke up to the reality that any notion of returning to live in Italy was now out of the question. And the second generation realized that they were American.

Most Italian Americans admired Mussolini and his Fascist Regime, which aimed at restoring Italy's ancient greatness and incidentally "made the trains run on time." But then again, most Americans admired Mussolini. The general news media and the *Chicago Tribune* had many positive things to say about the new Italy. The Mussolini government put a lot of resources into public relations aimed at the United States and it especially courted the leaders of the Italian-American community in Chicago. They responded enthusiastically, only to get the rug pulled out from under them when Italy declared war on the United States following the Pearl Harbor attack. Like their compatriots throughout North America, Chicago's Italians faced deep conflicting loyalties. Military experience exposed them to a wider range of life's possibilities.

On the whole, public opinion of the Italian immigrant in the 1920s was a negative one. Poverty, ignorance, black-hand crime, and Prohibition-related violence were the chief ingredients in the public image of Italians during that decade. Even the most sympathetic saw Italians in the city as suitable objects for social work, charity, and rehabilitation—perhaps a more negative image than the criminal stereotype. Nevertheless, in the mid-1920s, the Italians in Chicago still maintained their *Italianitá*: they retained their language, their family patterns, and their religious practices in the old neighborhoods even while they were becoming "Americanized" by their daily contacts with non-Italians (mostly immigrants themselves).

Mussolini came to power in Italy in 1922 and led Italy into fascism and a disastrous alliance with Hitler in World War II. Initially, Mussolini and fascism reinforced *Italianitá* among Chicago's Italians. In fact, the proudest moment in the history of Italians in Chicago came on July 15, 1933, when Italo Balbo's squadron of planes completed their transatlantic flight, landing in Lake Michigan as part of the World's Fair activities. With 100 crewmen in 24 airplanes, the Balbo expedition put the Italians in the forefront of aviation. The Chicago public and media regarded the event with almost as much enthusiasm as they had regarded the Lindbergh flight. The event and hoopla surrounding it put Italians on the front pages of the *Tribune*—in a positive light for change. The headlines read "Chicago Hails Balbo Fleet, Mighty Throngs Line Lake Shore; Cheer Happy Landing." There was a parade down Michigan Avenue, a reception at Fort Sheridan on the North Shore, a Soldier Field speech to an audience of 100,000, a presentation of a Sioux Indian head dress to Balbo, meetings with the mayor and the governor and other dignitaries, the unveiling of a Columbus statue, and the renaming of Eighth Street in Grant Park to "Balbo Drive."

The Italian community came out in full force to honor their hero. Balbo, an early and effective leader of Fascism in Italy, was greeted by fascist salutes and the *'Eia, Eia Alala'* mantra at an Italian-American banquet attended by 5,000 people in the Stevens (Conrad Hilton) Hotel. Under a huge backdrop of the images of Mussolini and the king of Italy, Balbo spoke with emotion, urging those who had endured the "tragic odyssey of emigration" to be both proud Italians and good Americans. This seemingly innocuous advice proved a lot easier to follow in 1933 than in 1941 when Italy and Mussolini became one of America's enemies in World War II.

A good number of Italian men, like young Gus Lazzarini, showed up in black shirts. Lazzarini was delighted when Consul General Giuseppe Castruccio picked him out of the crowd to translate some of the aviator's impromptu remarks. The glory of Balbo reflected well on the Italian community, welding them close to the Mussolini regime even while elevating their status in Chicago society.

The lone dissenting group was the Italian Socialist Federation (ISF), which hired an airplane to fly over the Century of Progress Fair and drop thousands of leaflets among the crowds. The leaflets condemned Balbo for his role in the murder of Italian Socialist Deputy Giacomo Matteotti. The ISF also blamed Balbo for "congratulating and protecting" the murderers of Reverend Don Minzoni of Argenta and they protested the fact that Cardinal Mundelein intended to preside over a mass in honor of Balbo—a man responsible for the murder of a priest. As a follow-up, someone (probably Egidio Clemente) sent an embarrassing "congratulatory" telegram to Balbo. As was the custom of the day, the master of ceremonies presented to the crowd proclamations and messages of congratulations. Obviously unaware of the significance of what he was doing, the emcee read aloud the bogus message that was signed "The Ghost of Don Minzoni, Arch Priest of Argenta," to the banquet guests. The organizers of the banquet were stunned and they moved quickly to screen additional telegrams. In yet another stunt, Clemente and Anthony Camboni led a midnight sortie that replaced the newly-erected Balbo Drive sign with a makeshift one that read "Don Minzoni Drive."

As colorful as the Socialist protests might have been, they did not change the fact that the Balbo visit to Chicago was an enormous public relations success for fascism in both the Italian and American communities. Years of planning for the Balbo flight by Chicago Consul General Castruccio had paid off. In addition to the Balbo flight, the Mussolini government made a broad and continuous effort to woo the Italian-American leadership and make them loyal to the fascist regime. When Mussolini patched up relations between the Italian government and the Catholic Church in February of 1929 with the famous Concordat, great celebrations were held at many Italian Catholic churches. In the agreement, the Italian government recognized the sovereignty of the Pope over Vatican City and the primacy of Catholicism as the state religion. In exchange, the Church accepted the legitimacy of the Italian government and its claim to the rest of Rome. At last it was possible to be both a good Catholic and an ardent Italian nationalist.

At St. Philip Benizi and Our Lady of Pompeii, church and government officials organized in each parish about a thousand parishioners and the banners of all the societies for a "Festa della Conciliazione fra la Chiesa e lo Stato Italiano" (A Feast of the Reconciliation between the Church and the Italian State). Photographers choreographed and took enormous group photos in front of each church to illustrate the unity and joy that the new agreement brought to the community. To view these photos, see the author's *Images of America: Italians in Chicago*. In the decade before World War II, most Italian clerics in Chicago could be depended upon to be cooperative with Italian fascist propaganda initiatives. Reportedly the Italian government routinely supplied fascist-oriented learning materials for Italian Catholic schools and youth groups.

In the 1930s, it was politically correct to admire Mussolini. Colonel Robert R. McCormick, publisher of the *Tribune*, was a big fan. Politicians attempting to appeal to Italian-American voters were not reluctant to pander to their audience with favorable references to Il Duce. It was only natural that the Sons of Italy and the Italo American National Union (the former Unione Siciliana) and their leaders George Spatuzza and Vincent Ferrara were among the staunchest supporters of Mussolini. Other initiatives calculated to ingratiate the Mussolini regime with the leadership of the Italian community included invitations to Italy, awards of merit, subsidies to friendly publications and cultural events, and the sponsorship of the *Balilla*, the Italian fascist version of the Boy Scouts. The consular office was no doubt kept busy recommending titles of "Commendatore" and "Cavaliere" friendly toward Mussolini's regime.

The consulate also diligently sent back reports on "subversive" anti-fascist Italian Americans. In an attempt to pressure Egidio Clemente, local fascist officials menacingly visited his mother in Trieste in an attempt to pressure Clemente to curtail his outspoken criticism in Chicago of the Mussolini Regime.

Mussolini's famous appeal to Italian women to contribute their gold wedding rings to help finance the fascist campaign to conquer Ethiopia was a success in Chicago. In return for the gold rings, the Italian government provided steel ones inscribed "Premier Benito Mussolini." According to the *Daily News*, almost 3,000 Italian-American women in Chicago who gave their gold were honored in a remarriage ceremony at the 132 Infantry Armory on the West Side on May 24, 1936. The couples, who had already contributed their gold rings months before, were to report to the armory, select a steel ring of the right size, then report to a priest who would bless the ceremony. Among the sponsors of the event were the Consul General Mario Carosi, the Sons of Italy, the IANU, Federated Italian War Veterans, and many well-known Italian Americans such as Peter Fosco, Lucy Palermo, Reverend Pasquale De Carlo, and many others.

Until Italy attacked France in 1940, open support for Mussolini in the Italian community was high. This event was one of the factors that led Lawrence Marino of the Italo American National Union and George Spatuzza of the Sons of Italy to send letters to their members urging them to participate in the Chicago *Herald American*'s "I am an American Day" on May 18, 1941, in Grant Park, six months before Pearl Harbor.

After Pearl Harbor, the second generation marched off to war. Roughly speaking, what might be called the second generation emerged in the period 1920–1940. Born in Chicago, educated according to American and/or Catholic standards, influenced by the Prohibition of the 1920s, tempered by the Depression, and tested by service in World War II, this group was often ambivalent about ethnicity. Though they had experienced the joys of Italian family life, middle-class America had always frowned on their parents' language and customs. Then came the war with Italy as an enemy.

It is difficult to provide an accurate estimate of the number of Chicago Italians who served in the military during World War II. Italian immigration peaked in 1907 and 1914. Immigrants were young adults who probably married a few years after reaching Chicago, thus starting families by 1920. All of the males who were born to this peak immigrant group would have been of draft age in the 1940s. The Italian population was about 250,000 and if only 10 percent of that number ended up in the service, it was still 25,000. The experiences of these impressionable young men during the war were the most dangerous, most exciting, and most educational they would have in their lives.

Reminiscing a half century later at the Italian Cultural Center in 1995, Mike Palello gave an eyewitness account of the attack on Pearl Harbor. Duke Masaro spoke of being wounded and receiving a Bronze Star at Beauganville in the Philippines. Joe Tolitano related an incident at Fort Knox that ended in a tussle when another soldier called him a "Dago." Tom Barrata explained that his mother's mail in Chicago came under surveillance when he inadvertently revealed his unit's location in a letter back home. And Tony Scariano told of his experiences behind enemy lines in Italy with the OSS.

In general, the community at home gave great recognition to the families of servicemen. Parents, especially mothers, who could barely speak English, found themselves at events with flags and bands honored by mayors and military officers for their patriotic loyalty to the United States. Mothers displayed stars in their windows indicating the number of their children in the military. A Gold Star indicated that a family member had been killed in action. Neighbors erected on corner lots honor rolls of the boys from that neighborhood who were serving their country. And many merchants used their display windows to exhibit photographs of townspeople serving in the various branches of the military.

The Italian American Chamber of Commerce sponsored "Spaghetti Nights" for servicemen in uniform who happened to be traveling through in the downtown area. As mentioned earlier, the St. Anthony *Broadcast* and similar newsletters sent information about the hometown boys to their buddies around the world. Italian publications ran free advertisements for the Red Cross and various war bond drives.

In World War II, the people and events that influenced the Italian community in that era dramatize the most important transition in the history of the group. Although a number of Italian fascists throughout the United States were arrested and quite a few California Italians had their lives disrupted by government agents, only six or eight were taken into custody in the Chicago area. At this point no grossly unjust treatment of Italians suspected of espionage had surfaced in Chicago.

According to John Antognoli, a chamber officer in that era, federal agents did seize the files and office machines of the Italian American Chamber of Commerce and interrogated him and the group's other officers. Italian immigrants who were not yet U.S. citizens were required to register as enemy aliens at their local post office. In Chicago Heights, hundreds of Italians, mostly women, crowded the post office to submit their Alien Registration forms. Partly as a strategy to gain full support from Italian Americans for the war, on Columbus Day 1942, less than a year after Pearl Harbor, U.S. Attorney General Francis Biddle removed Italians from the enemy alien classification. Another motivation for this action was that Italian "Enemy Aliens" were much more likely to be Gold Star Mothers than fascist spies.

On the homefront, vocal support for the fascist regime died out, but the federal government wanted more from Italians. Being 100 percent American was not enough. They wanted Italian Americans to be outspokenly 100 percent anti-fascist. The government wanted Italian-American leaders to guide the Italian population toward outright repudiation of Mussolini and the fascist regime. The Office of War Information (OWI) was apparently troubled that the pre-war fascists in Chicago and elsewhere were lukewarm in their support for the United States and its allies. These elements continued to criticize British policy and to belittle the potential of the Russians to withstand German invasion. Their war bond drives were often aimed at supplying noncombatant equipment such as ambulances to the war effort. And they boycotted the Italian-American anti-fascist speeches and rallies sponsored by the Mazzini Society.

In order to intensify and unify public opinion in support of the war and as a tactic in the psychological war with Italy, government agents tried to maneuver Italian-American leaders to publicly embrace the arguments that the Italian Socialist Federation had been preaching for 20 years. In Chicago, the OWI found a willing partner in Judge George Quilici.

George Quilici was a Democrat and an articulate anti-fascist who wasn't a socialist. Therefore, he became the perfect choice to lead the Italian community during World War II. According to Miller and Panofsky, Quilici's father came to Chicago in 1893 from Tuscany and built up a series of small businesses. He was an itinerant knife sharpener, then an ice cream vendor with a small chain of stores, and then he went into the movie theatre business. The elder Quilici's fast track immigrant success afforded young George the opportunity to attend De Paul University, then Marshall Law School. He served in a U.S. combat unit during World War I, then came back to Chicago to practice law. He was among the organizers of the Justinian Society of Lawyers in 1921. Quilici was also among the founders of the Mazzini Society in the early 1930s. The main purpose of this club was to combat fascism. Once the war began, its aim was to replace fascism with a republican form of government in postwar Italy.

Elected municipal judge in 1940, Quilici was a prime mover in the formation of the Italian American Victory Council and was chosen as its chair. Their motto was "Victory for America—Freedom for Italy." Though it might seem like a simple task to bring together 50 or so ethnic organizations to express their patriotism at rallies and sell war bonds, pre-war rivalries surfaced almost immediately. The socialists and other anti-fascists wanted to control the council as a reward for being right about Mussolini. And they wanted to punish the mainline fraternal groups who had been in Mussolini's pocket before Pearl Harbor. Unfortunately, the mainline organizations represented the vast majority of the Italians in Chicago compared to the well-informed and intense socialist contingent in the city. The OWI agent in charge, Renzo Sereno, ultimately demoralized the socialists as he pressured Quilici to bend over backwards to make the former pro-fascists full partners in the victory council. Of course, since the main objective was unity and support for the American war effort, there was no way that the mainline organizations could be ignored. The victory council needed to use those leaders whether or not they had been pro-fascist in order to reach the masses. And despite the grumbling of the left about the "Gianni-come-latelys," the inclusive strategy worked; the rallies were well attended, war bonds sold successfully, and the former fascists had been co-opted to the American cause. In April 1942, George Quilici explained it to the *Herald American* it more polite terms, "Groups that never before would sit down together in the same room for any purpose are uniting in this cause. We represent nearly all shades of opinion."

The Chicago Italian American Victory Council participated in a program sponsored by the OWI to broadcast, via short-wave radio messages by Italian Americans, urging the Italian people to welcome invading American forces. In his radio address, Quilici stressed that the Italian American Victory Council made a distinction between the Italian government and the Italian people. He assured his Italian audience that the council would work tirelessly to safeguard the future of Italy after the fall of fascism. He urged them to separate themselves from the fascist regime. George Spatuzza's statement targeted the people of his home town Ragusa, which was in the process of occupation by American troops. "Citizens of my native town, please listen to the appeal of your far away brother. Co-operate with the armies of the United Nations. Look not upon them as enemies, but as liberators." Tony Gattone, using the Sicilian dialect, recorded a similar message directed to his old friends in Catania, reassuring them that the Americans did not wish to harm the Italian people but came to liberate them from the German danger.

The war in Italy was very complicated. As Allied forces began to invade, Mussolini was forced to resign and was placed under arrest on July 25, 1943, leaving the Italian government in the hands of General Pietro Badoglio and King Victor Emmanuel. When the King and Badoglio surrendered to the Allies in September 1943, Italy fell into anarchy. Italy's German allies swept into Italy to prevent a complete collapse. Thus, parts of Italy were occupied by both their former ally from the north (the Germans) and their enemies from the south (the Americans and the British).

Even after his political fall from grace, Mussolini was still not out of the picture. He was rescued by the German forces from imprisonment and set up as puppet ruler of the "Republic of Salo" in northern Italy. In April 1945, shortly before the end of the war, Mussolini was caught by Italian partisans and executed.

In July of 1943, when Mussolini fell from power, Chicago newspaper reporters rushed out to get quotes from Italian Americans about the good news. Anti-fascist Professor Gaetano Borghese, of the University of Chicago, was not satisfied because he had no confidence in either the king or the general. George Spatuzza, of the Sons of Italy, shed tears of joy. Attorney Ellidor Libonati, of the American Legion, who had met Badoglio in 1920, expressed confidence in him. Reverend De Carlo was pleased that the resignation made an opening for the American Army to be used by God to do good in Italy. Led by their president, Anthony Iacculo, 500 happy Italians celebrated Mussolini's ouster at the Societá Operai Agricola meeting on Taylor Street as they waved American flags and sang patriotic songs.

The biggest event sponsored by the IAVC came on Sunday, August 29, 1943, when it staged the "Greater Chicago Italian American Day" celebration at the Grant Park Band Shell. The letterhead featured the names of 75 political figures and club presidents. Honorary Chair Peter Fosco, General Chair George Quilici, and War Bond Chair N.J. Bonelli signed this invitation to this "greatest rally of all time." A crowd of 10,000 came out to see film stars Leo Carrillo (the Cisco Kid) and Victor Mature, a Swiss-Italian, and opera diva Vivian della Chiesa. Bond sales for that day reached $1 million. Speakers included Senator Scott Lucas, Governor Dwight Green, Bishop Bernard Shield, Quilici, Spatuzza, and Marino. Only Spatuzza addressed the crowd in Italian.

Exactly a month after the rally Italy surrendered. That of course did not end the fighting nor did it diminish the need for the IAVC. For the next few years, the council focused on getting relief for wartorn Italy. From 1944 onward they worked through Catholic Relief and American Relief for Italy, Incorporated. The Chicago Italian American Chamber of Commerce (CIACC) put out calls for members to help the monastery of the Clarisse in Rome. In September 1945 they ran appeals for donations for trucks for Italy, collecting a total of $14,000, or enough to buy seven trucks. Chicago Italians supported the efforts of Dr. Nicola Emanuele of Ashland and Roosevelt Road who headed up a committee along with Piero Faò to get medical aid to Italy. The Sons of Italy's Peter Porzio ran a campaign to buy milk for undernourished Italian children. The United National Clothing Collection for Oversea War Relief begged Italians and others to clean out their clothes closets to help the 125 million people in wartorn Europe. In the postwar era, the CIACC continued to lobby for stepped-up food relief shipments for both humanitarian and political reasons. Angry, hungry Italians would turn to communism.

The single most important Chicago Italian involved with World War II didn't spend much time in Chicago. Chicago Italian Americans claim Enrico Fermi (1901–1954) as one of their heroes. Fermi was the émigré physicist who left in 1939 to collect a Nobel Prize, never to return to fascist Italy. His was an act of protest against Mussolini's alliance with Hitler and against maltreatment of Jews. Fermi's wife, Laura, was Jewish. She has written several books about her life with Fermi as he led a team in New York, Chicago, then New Mexico in their successful attempt to create an atomic chain reaction. Today a sculpture by Henry Moore marks the spot where, underneath the University of Chicago Stagg Field, on December 2, 1942 Fermi's team achieved the first chain reaction. The event was marked by two Italian-oriented acts. First, the message was sent to authorities, "The Italian navigator has reached the New World." Second, someone broke out a bottle of Chianti wine and everyone toasted their success, somewhat relieved that the chain reaction hadn't blown up the whole city. Some writers have claimed that Fermi also made a derogatory remark about Hitler and how the supposed inferior race had beaten the Arian race to the punch on atomic energy. The atomic bomb hastened the conclusion of World War II and undoubtedly saved the lives of thousands of Americans.

While Fermi's place in world history is clear, his place in the history of Chicago Italian Americans is not. He was an émigré who only spent a few years total in Chicago, mostly in the lab or with his colleagues before his death in 1954 from stomach cancer (probably induced by radiation). Whether he ever had time to shop at the Conte di Savoia deli or attend an operetta in Roseland is not known. On the other hand, he did bring a group of colleagues like physicists Emilio Segrè and Ugo Fano, who spent many years at the University of Chicago. In fact, there has been a strong and continuous colony of Italian faculty and researchers in a variety of disciplines at the University of Chicago for many years. Finally, the FermiLab stands as a constant symbol of Italian achievement that should swell the pride of Italian Americans at least as much as Balbo's Flight.

In appreciation for service in World War II, Congress passed the G.I. Bill, which opened up to Italian Americans the first real opportunities for a college education. Many also took advantage of vocational training in the G.I. Bill. The program also included access to low-interest housing loans, a godsend to newly married couples who had been forced to live with their parents during the postwar housing shortage.

The perhaps unintended consequence of these and other governmental policies, such as urban renewal, public housing projects, and the creation of the interstate highways and urban expressways, combined to undermine the inner-city neighborhoods.

It is doubtful that any Chicago ethnic community was damaged as greatly by government policies during that period as was the Italian-American community. First, there was the building of the Cabrini-Green housing project, which began during the war. It impacted the Near North Side Sicilian enclave in the 1940s and 1950s. Then came the construction of the expressway system on the near South, West, and Northwest Sides, which dislodged additional Italian (and other ethnic) families and institutions, including the church and the new school of the Holy Guardian Angel at the Dan Ryan Expressway and Forquer Street.

The exodus of Italians was west to Austin and along Grand Avenue, eventually reaching Harlem Avenue. In the early 1960s, the first Mayor Daley determined to build the new Chicago branch of the University of Illinois in the Taylor Street neighborhood. This meant that approximately one square mile of the heavily Italian community, including 13 buildings of the Hull House complex, had to be razed. Within a decade, the Roseland-Pullman Italian community fell victim to residential change accelerated by real estate block busters who profited from the expansion of the Black South Side by scaring

Italian-American residents into abandoning their neighborhood and their new Church of St. Anthony of Padua.

After 1960, it became harder to just be an Italian American in an old Italian neighborhood. In the outer neighborhoods and the suburbs you had to work at being and staying Italian American. The overall result of all the positive and negative urban forces at work during the post–World War II era was that, except for a few noteworthy pockets of Italian settlement, Chicago's old Little Italies were destroyed. With them have gone the material culture of their neighborhoods, the sense of identity, and the feeling of security that the continuity and customs and familiar faces of the old neighborhood offered. And whatever political power the Italians could muster on the basis of geographic concentration was also undermined. Henceforth there could be no geographic base for the community. The community identity that survived had to be founded instead on a community of interest based almost entirely on voluntary associations and self-conscious identification with Italian-ness.

Chapter Eight

ITALIAN-AMERICAN ETHNIC ORGANIZATIONAL LIFE SINCE WORLD WAR II

The 2000 census reported 543,498 people in Illinois whose first ancestry is Italian and 188,325 whose second ancestry is Italian. In Cook County there are 327,011 Italian Americans or 6.1 percent of the population. The Chicago figure is 191,998 or 6.6 percent of the population. The Italian population in DuPage County is 108,862 and Lake County, 45,060.

For Italian Americans in the start of the twenty-first century, the western suburbs are where it's at. The Chicago suburbs with the highest percentage of Italian-American population are as follows: Elmwood Park 28.7 percent (7,293), Norridge 25.5 percent (3,740), Hinsdale 23.5 percent (4,100), Highwood 22.6 percent (922), Elmhurst 21.5 percent (9,236), Westchester 20.9 percent (3,483), Bloomingdale 20.7 percent (4,471), Melrose Park 18.8 percent (4,368), Barrington Hills 17.5 percent (728), Elk Grove Village 17.1 percent (5,947), Darien 14.8 percent (3,402), Franklin Park 13 percent (2,536), Burr Ridge 12.2 percent (1,257), Alsip 11.8 percent (2,338), Chicago Heights 11.4 percent (3,757).

Since World War II the Italian-American horizon in Chicago has been filled with hundreds of clubs and organizations that reinforce and promote Italian identity. Attaining the final goal of respect is the stated or unstated purpose of the hundreds of voluntary associations that Italians have formed. Organized around religious, professional, recreational, charitable, social, educational, and cultural agendas, these groups have performed many good works. They contribute funds to worthy causes like Villa Scalabrini and the Italian Cultural Center. They have provided hundreds of small scholarships to young people. And these organizations provide leadership training. But more important than the good they do is the recognition that these organizations have brought to their leaders and their members. With so many small organizations around, everyone had the opportunity to become president or chair or some kind of officer with a respected title. It is in this kind of manageable social matrix that ethnics and non-ethnics alike can find the fellowship, recognition, prestige, and respect that most people find so elusive in the larger social arena of the metropolis with its seven million inhabitants. For Italian Americans, community events were the place to know people and to be known. The children and the grandchildren of the *paesani* were able to create a community, much different from the earlier immigrant colonies of the inner city and much less Italian. With the Italian language fading and first-hand memories of the old country all but gone, Chicagoland Italians made their way toward their ethnic identity as Italian Americans.

In the late 1940s the Italian Welfare Council (IWC) emerged and made a brief bid for leadership of Chicago's Italian-American community, focusing on children's programming and an ill fated attempt to permanently establish an old people's home at Pistakee Bay (near McHenry, Illinois) where the group also operated the Jolly Boys and Girls Camp. In 1949, the IWC ran a half dozen two-week camps for 200 young people in each session. The list of prominent Italian leaders who were officers and directors associated with the IWC in the period from 1945 to about 1952 included Anthony Sorrentino (executive director), Frank Chesrow, Horatio Tocco, Professor Joseph Fucilla of Northwestern University, Joseph R. Salerno (a candidate for the state senate in 1950), Dario Toffenetti, Vincent Ferrarra, Adam Vignola, Dr. Eugene Chesrow, Frank Annunzio, Mrs. Rose Ferinacci, Peter Fosco, and James Adducci. After the Joint Civic Committee was formed, the organization dissolved and its funds were contributed to the Damon Runyan Cancer Fund.

Pre-eminent among postwar organizations was the Joint Civic Committee of Italian Americans (JCCIA). It was established in 1952 in response to an effort by the Republican State Central Committee to drop Emil Caliendo from the electoral ticket (as explained previously in the section on Italians in politics). To combat this gross injustice, leaders from a variety of organizations formed the JCCIA as a federation to fight the major Italian-American problem: defamation. The organizational structure was very similar to that of the Italian American Victory Council. Among the early presidents of the JCCIA were attorney Joseph Barbera (1952–1960), attorney Peter Scalise, wine merchant Anthony Paterno, IANU leader Vincent Ferrara, shoe-repair magnate Joseph Tolitano, and union leader James E. Coli. For most of its history, the JCCIA maintained a downtown office.

Despite some flaws in its claim to be a federated umbrella organization, the JCCIA is generally conceded by the media and the political establishment to be the spokesman for the Chicago Italian-American community. Of key importance to the success and continuity of the JCCIA were the 30 years of diligent work of its executive director Anthony Sorrentino (one-time director of the Illinois Department of Delinquency Prevention) and the group's secretary, Marie Pallelo. Sorrentino's *Organizing the Ethnic Community* provides an exhaustive record of the JCCIA's history from 1952 to 1995. Oriented toward the regular Democratic Party, the officially nonpartisan JCCIA derived a good deal of its clout from the fact that its major patron was Congressman Frank Annunzio.

The JCCIA's Anti-Defamation Committee (later called the Human Relations Committee) used an effective combination of quiet influence, outraged protest, and award-giving flattery to nudge the news media toward more objective coverage of Italian Americans. Their major achievement has been to convince the news media to use the neutral term "organized crime" instead of automatically referring to criminal activity with Italian words such as "Mafia" and "Cosa Nostra." The JCCIA at various times has conducted campaigns against *The Untouchables*, *The Godfather*, insulting television commercials, and celebrities and journalists who make belittling remarks about Italians. The biggest challenge has been to get the public to understand that stereotypical portrayal of Italian Americans is just as damaging to Italian Americans as is the use of negative stereotypes regarding minorities.

Since 1972 the JCCIA has given the Dante Award to high profile Chicago print and media journalists who exhibited (and hopefully would continue to exhibit) fairness in their coverage of Italian-American issues and personalities. In the 1980s and 1990s, public relations professional Dominic Di Frisco used his talents to get better press for Italian Americans in Chicago and to protest unfair treatment of them. Di Frisco served an extended four years term as JCCIA president in the early 1990s and through his television appearances and *Fra Noi* column won wide approval as an articulate spokesman for Chicago Italians.

The most important annual function of the JCCIA continues to be the Columbus Day Parade, which it has sponsored since the JCCIA was organized in 1952. The JCCIA campaigned vigorously to have the State of Illinois declare Columbus Day a legal holiday in 1963 and a public school holiday in 1970. In 1971 Congressman Annunzio and New Jersey Congressman Peter Rodino successfully spearheaded a campaign to get the federal government to adopt Columbus Day as a national (Monday) holiday.

Because the parade takes place about three weeks before November elections, it attracts almost every politician in the state regardless of race, ethnicity, or party—jostling each other for positions in the front row. Like the old May Day Parades in Red Square, the Columbus Day event shows off the Italian community's "big guns," its power and its influence. National personalities who have appeared in the parade include Pat Nixon, Jimmy Carter, Senator Pete Domenici, and Ohio Governor Richard Celeste. Led for many years by perennial grand marshal Marco de Stefano, the 150-unit parade included high school bands and floats and marching delegations representing Italian businesses and organizations, as well as politicians and businesses wishing to ingratiate themselves with the Italian target market. And, despite the politically-correct deconstruction of Columbus by academics and Native Americans, the parade marches on.

The other major event sponsored by the JCCIA is a hotel banquet/fundraiser in honor of such luminaries as Mayor Jane Byrne, Alderman Edward Vrdolyak, and various powerful Italian-American labor leaders. In the early 1960s, the JCCIA forged an alliance with Villa Scalabrini and the *Fra Noi* that gave increased credibility to all concerned. Together, the agencies have sponsored a dizzying array of cultural, folkloric, and social events ranging from Italian language classes to debutante balls. One of the most impressive cultural achievements of this coalition was the presentation in 1962 and 1963 of "Sojourn in Italy," a 21-week lecture series on Italian culture. State Representative Victor Arrigo, Father Salvatore DiVita, attorneys Nello Ori and Maurice Marchello, Professor Joseph Cinquino, Judge George Quilici, and others made presentations on cuisine, architecture, literature, art, and the regions of Italy. Attendance at the downtown center of De Paul University sometimes reached 500.

A "secret weapon" of the JCCIA was the Women's Division. Formed in 1966 with the help of educator Mary Ellen Battinich, this organization and the West Suburban branch provided a steady stream of volunteers and financial contributions that enabled the JCCIA to move beyond the scope of a one-issue organization. The JCCIA benefited enormously from the years of effort by such people as: Jean Bruno, Rose Flood, Elena Jo Frigoletti, Carolyn Lucchese, Ann Sorrentino, Mary Spallitta, Bonnie Tisci, Ann Yelmini, Norma Battisti, Annette Salvatore, Lillia Juarez, and Tena Amico. Serafina Ferrara, who owned Ferrara Pastry and was so well-known for her generosity that people call her "The Angel of Taylor Street," also played a key role in helping the Women's Division. From all accounts their meetings were more business-like and their committees more participatory than those of the men's division.

The Women's Division multiplied the number of events sponsored by the JCCIA to include fashion shows, the Folk Fair, an authentic costume committee, and an annual Italian Heritage Ball and Cotillion. Pauline Jo Cusimano and her sister Marilyn Fredericks recruited adults, teenagers, and children and taught them ethnic dances and various drills. The children's group, the Italianettes, for many years appeared at various Italian events like Festa Italiana and "Christmas Around the World" at the Museum of Science and Industry.

In 2003 the JCCIA finally embraced their secret weapon and elected Joanne Spata as its first female president. She is dedicated to bringing younger and newer groups into the organization. One of those groups, FIERI (meaning the Proud Ones), appeared in Chicago in the 1990s and is made up of mostly college-educated professionals under 39. There are affiliates in New York and other cities and the organization holds national conferences that focus on leadership development and cultural issues.

The oldest Italian-American organizations are the *paesani*-based mutual benefit societies. These groups provided funeral benefits and other minor social assistance to the new immigrants and developed to include social activities and patron saint celebrations. Because the social security system replaced many of the insurance functions of these organization and because many of the societies were actuarially unsound (most members were in the same age cohort), most *societé di mutuo soccorso* fell by the wayside. Among those maintaining death benefits are: Campobello di Mazzara Social Club, Societá Amasenese of Chicago Heights, Marchegiani Society of Chicago Heights, Alleanza Riciglianese, and Societá Modenese di Mutuo Soccorso.

The most dramatic evidence of the retention of ethnicity among Chicago's Italian Americans has historically been demonstrated in the religious street festivals. Italians parading the graven images laden with money pinned to their garments through the streets were shocking to American Protestants, and not a little disturbing to the Irish hierarchy and even some Italian priests. There have been occasional disputes between lay leaders and pastors over management of the festivals. One would have thought that such folk practices as bargaining with a saint to receive favors would have been an early casualty of Americanization. And indeed, 20 years ago the number of such feasts had dwindled to a handful. But in recent times there has been a resurgence in the number and intensity of these celebrations. In the 1920s one could attend a different *festa* each Sunday in the summer at the Sicilian St. Philip Benizi Church; in the 1980s one could still attend a *festa* each Sunday, but one would have to travel around the whole Chicago metropolitan area do it. Because neighborhoods changed and churches closed, many festivals had to search for new locations.

The July 1987 *Fra Noi* contained a pull-out section detailing some 20 feasts, big and small, in the Chicago area. The Feast of Our Lady of Mount Carmel, which has been celebrated in mid-July in Melrose Park since the 1890s, and the Feast of Santissima Maria Lauretana, which originated at St. Philip Benizi in 1900 and is now celebrated at Harlem and Cermak, are the two largest feasts, each drawing up to 100,000 people over their multi-day run.

The Feast of San Francesco di Paola, held on the grounds of Casa Italia (Italian Cultural Center) in Stone Park, was begun in the 1980s by Father Roberto

Simionato at the behest of postwar immigrants from Calabria and has fast become one of the most spirited events on the Italian-American horizon. The Calabrian Regional government has several times provided topnotch entertainers, and the feast in the second week of August is the most popular event of the year at the Casa Italia campus. For more information on the Lauretana and San Francesco feasts, refer to the author's *Voices in America: Italians in Chicago.*

In the 1980s the summer feast line up and their approximate dates also included: San Antonio on June 13 at St. Anthony of Padua; Santa Liberata, June l0, St. Ferdinand Church; Our Lady of Mount Carmel, July 15, Melrose Park; Our Lady of Mount Carmel, July 15, Chicago Ridge; Tutti Santi, July 20, Armour Square; St. John Bosco, July 26, Italian Cultural Center; San Rocco Di Modugno, August 26, Santa Maria Addolorata Church; San Donatus, August 10, Blue Island; San Fancesco di Paola, August 10, Italian Cultural Center; San Lorenzo, August 10, Chicago Heights; San Rocco di Potenza, August 12, Holy Rosary Church; Santa Maria del Pozzo, August 26, Villa Scalabrini; Santissima Maria Lauretana, September 5, Harlem & Cermak; Santa Maria Incoronata, September 12, Chinatown; San Gennaro, September 19, Our Lady of Pompeii; Crosifisso di Rutgliano, September 23, St. Ferdinand Church.

Also notable are the smaller feasts that have either been revived or established in the past few decades. *Paesani*-based organizations also support patron saint festivities on behalf of Beato Giovanni Liccio (Caccamo), Maria Santissima Della Croce (Triggiano, Bari), San Biagio Platani (San Biagio, Agrigento), San Francesco di Paolo (Calabria), San Giuseppe (Casteldaccia, Sicily and Sannicandro, Bari), San Leoluca (Corleone), San Rocco (Modugno, Bari; Simbario, Catanzaro, Potenza, Lucania, and Valenzano, Bari), Sant'Amatore (Cellamare, Bari), Santa Fara (Cinisi, Palermo), and the San Lorenzo Feast (Amaseno) in Chicago Heights.

And the list continues: the Society Maria Santissima del Pozzo (Capurso, Bari); La Societá Originale Santa Rosalia, (Campofelice di Roccella); La Societá San Gennaro (Napoli) in the Taylor Street community; La Societá Santo Stefano e San Vincenzo Martiri, (Castel San J Vincenzo, Isernia); La Societá Unione Progresso e Civilita di Simbario (Catanzaro, Calabria); the St. Angelo Muxaro Club; (Raiano, Abruzzi); Maria Santissima della Salute (Ambrogio, Palermo); *Associazione di San Giuseppe* (Sannicandro, Bari); *Maria Santissima Incoronata e San Cristoforo* (Ricigliano); Saint Mary of Sambuca Society (Palermo); San Giovanni Bosco Society of Ciminna (Sicily); San Giuseppe di Casteldaccia Society (Palermo); *La Societá Sant'Amatore* (Cellamare, Bari); the Santa Liberata Club (Pizzone, Isernia); *La Societá della Provvidenza* (Nicosia, Enna); *La Societá di Maria Santissima di Constantinopoli* (Bari);

Maria Santissima Addolorata, patron of Mola di Bari; *M.S. Santa Caterina Villarmosa* (Caltanissetta); *La Societá Maria Santissima del Pozzo* (Capurso, Bari).

These long, long lists are overwhelming evidence of the loyalty of generations of Italians in Chicago to ancient religious, family, clan, and ethnic traditions and values. Sicilian and Baresi towns of origin obviously lead the way in the number of patron saint feasts celebrated in Chicago. The general list suggests the rich texture of the sense of community rooted in practices that might have been expected to die out generations ago.

Religious events, or these *paesani*/clan/neighborhood activities, have mixed charitable and commercial purposes, but few who attend can fail to appreciate the symbolism, the tradition, and the sincerity of the faithful. In the twenty-first century, *campanilismo*, or loyalty to town of origin, after several generations is remarkable. Ethnicity is nothing if not symbolic, and the *feste* themselves, laden with ancient symbolism, proclaim a convincing challenge to all who would dismiss the authenticity of Italian-American ethnicity in Chicago today.

Perhaps the organizations that have shown the most energy in the past two decades are those based on region of origin. Composed mainly of post–World War II immigrants who have maintained close ties to their homeland, the regional associations are supported and encouraged by regional government tourism and culture officials. Politicians in Italy have also shown higher interest in emigrants because of new regulations concerning duel citizenship that extend some voting rights to Italians abroad. Regional officials have arranged cultural exchanges and offered low cost group excursions and other benefits to their co-*regionali*.

Thus, by the early 1990s the list of regional associations included the Associazione Regionale Pugliese in America (ARPA), the Associazione Regionale Siciliana, Associazione Regionale Campania, the Lucchesi nel Mondo, the Molisani nel Mondo, the Piemontesi nel Mondo, the Sicilian American Cultural Association, the Veneti nel Mondo, and a fledgling Associazzione Laziali del Nord America.

The oldest branched fraternal group in Chicago is the Italo American National Union (IANU). It was founded in 1895 as the Unione Siciliana and played an important leadership role in the 1930s and 1940s. Especially notable were the letter writing campaigns in 1947 and 1953 warning Italian relatives of the dangers of communism and extolling the virtues of the American system. Possibly as a response to McCarthyism, the IANU also pledged in 1953 to expand its citizenship and Americanization programs through its members in various parts of the midwest. It currently has 19 chapters in northeast Illinois and northwest Indiana and merged in 1991 with the Italian Sons and Daughters of America (ISDA) based in Pittsburgh.

The Sons of Italy statewide organization continues to be a major player on the Chicago scene. It has a dozen affiliates in the Chicago area and its first female president, Giovanna Verdecchia, created a strong alliance with Consul General Enrico Granara to lobby for state grants for Italian language instruction.

The National Italian American Sports Hall of Fame (NIASHF) combines love of sport with love of one's ethnicity to produce an appealing program that has drawn wide interest. The organization in the mid-1990s boasted of nearly 5,000 members in 18 chapters across the country. This mega-movement was started in 1977 when George Randazzo organized a fundraising dinner that featured Italian-American boxers. He latched onto the idea of a boxing hall of fame, then soon expanded it to include all sports. Randazzo opened a model exhibit in a storefront in Elmwood Park in 1978. His idea had enormous appeal and Randazzo was a master at networking. Soon he had the support of Tommy Lasorda, Yogi Berra, and then, over time, nearly 200 Hall of Fame inductees and all their friends and admirers. President Carter even dropped in on the 1980 awards dinner.

In the 1980s the storefront moved to a handsome, but remote, Arlington Heights site and finally in 2003 the IASHF moved into a state of the art 44,000-square foot museum building on land donated by the City of Chicago on Taylor Street. The new museum is expected to attract a broad audience of sports fans and general tourists in addition to Italian Americans. Across the street from the building is a magnificent sculpture of "Joltin' Joe" DiMaggio in full swing.

On a smaller scale, the Italian Cultural Center conducts a program more oriented to the Italian-American market. Now integrated with the Casa Italia, the Center provides language classes for children and adults, sponsors the Josephine LiPuma Vocal Scholarship program, and maintains a library, art gallery, historic photo exhibit, the Savoia scale model Vatican exhibit, and a recording studio. The Center has also given a forum to dozens of creative Italian-American writers, painters, sculptors, and film makers. Fred Gardaphé of Melrose Park, who currently heads up an Italian American Studies program at SUNY–Stony Brook, has made many presentations at the Center and was briefly an officer. The Center has sponsored dozens of art exhibits and awarded thousands of dollars in prize money to budding Italian-American artists like Christopher Buoscio and established artists like watercolorist Luigi Sampiere. Sculptors Virginio Ferrari, Mario Spampinato, Vito Davi, and Robert Buono exhibited their works over the years. And well-known filmmaker Tom Pallazolo participated in a number of Cultural Center

Art Shows. Italian language performers and poets who have presented programs include Gino and Maria Nuccio, folk singer Pompeo Stillo, Lionel Bottari, autobiographer Vincenzo Lettieri, and poet Pietro Bertucelli.

Central to organizational life since World War II is *Fra Noi*. Under the editorship of Paul Basile for the past 13 years, a key theme has been expansion. Its monthly editions reflect and promote the myriad activities of Chicago Italians. In 1998, with the advent of lay control of the whole Sacred Heart Seminary Campus, Italian organizations obtained direct access to valuable capital resources. This included the Cultural Center, a gym/auditorium, a dormitory, a former convent, a chapel, outdoor pavilion, and a shrine. And though some of them needed major repairs, the acquisition was a windfall for Italian-American organizations.

Paul Basile was also entrusted with the task of developing Casa Italia to be the physical focal center of Italian-American organizational life. The Board of Directors, which includes Anthony Fornelli, Renato Turano, Paul Butera, and many other leading Italian businessmen, has charged Basile with attracting as many organizations as possible to make Casa Italia their home base. State Senator James DeLeo and State Representative Angelo "Skip" Saviano pitched in by awarding a total of $350,000 in Illinois First grant money for infrastructure improvements on aspects of the Casa Italia campus that could be shared with the general public. In 2002 the Board of Directors of the Casa Italia was doubled in size and additional staff members were hired to assist Basile.

The Maroons Soccer Club is another example of the combined power of sports and ethnicity. The first Italian-American soccer team, "Italy Soccer Club," was organized in a meeting room at the Chicago Commons Settlement House in 1929 by Dominick Passaglia, Umberto Mugnaini, Dr. Joseph Safford, Charles Verni, Marino Mazzei, and Amedeo Moschioni. Possibly influenced by the heightened nationalism of fascist Italy, the formation of the team united Italian players who had previously played for nationalities. This combination of love of sport and pride in the Italian nationality kept the Maroons going strong under a series of names and sponsorships. Vital to their success was support from the Mazzini-Verdi Club, restaurateur George Portesi, Narciso "Bimbo" Bianchi, Leonard Fricano, Pietro Cavallini, Rago Brothers Funeral Home, De Luxe Ice Cream, Alitalia, Frank Grimaldi, Gus Lazzerini, Silvio Stefani, and many others. The establishment of their own headquarters in Elmwood Park, the development of soccer programs for boys and girls at all levels, and the growing popularity of soccer seem to assure the future of the Maroons.

In Chicago, as in other cities in the 1980s and 1990s, the commercialized Festa Italiana featured big-name Italian-American entertainers, food, art, and Sunday mass on the Lakefront. The organizers, Anthony Fornelli and his Amerital Unico, for 15 years produced at a variety of lakefront locations Chicago's Festa Italiana. Some years the attendance reached close to 100,000 people. The target audience was the Italian community, the general public, and the traveling public staying in the downtown hotels. The "Kiss me, I'm Italian!" spirit of the event projected a positive image of the ethnic group. The financial benefits for the various vendors, most of whom were Italian business owners, were sometimes enormous. Unico used the proceeds (over $1 million over the 15-year run) to encourage and support organizations like the Italian Cultural Center, the Cooley's Anemia Foundation, the Villa Scalabrini, and a variety of Italian heritage institutions and other charitable activities, thereby intensifying and perpetuating the identification of all participants with things Italian. Unfortunately, Unico's Festa was plagued by bad weather and it suffered logistic nightmares when it was forced to change its location four or five times in its 15 years.

Though most of the major Italian-American organizations are city wide, a relatively new neighborhood-based organization emerged in the mid-1980s that has creatively combined ethnic identity with other urban forces, such as political patronage, fear of neighborhood racial change, professional public relations tactics, and *paesani*-type loyalty, to produce the Old Neighborhood Italian American Club (ONIAC). The group is focused on the Chinatown, Bridgeport, and Armour Square areas of the near South Side. Using the slogan "Basta!" (enough), the group has picketed the local NBC-TV affiliate, sponsored a parade and free picnic, organized a multi-saint festa, sponsored city-wide annual dinners, and generally injected militant rhetoric into what is usually regarded as an "Uncle Tommaso" (Uncle Tom) Italian-American style. In the late 1980s, ONIAC seemed to be challenging the JCCIA for the leadership of the Italian community, but after one of its leading members was imprisoned on racketeering charges, ONIAC's activities seemed to be confined to the neighborhood, and prospects of organizing the entire community on the militant model of ONIAC diminished sharply. In recent years ONIAC has settled into a quieter role as a health club with monthly dinner meetings.

Italian-American business and professional groups do for their members what the Rotary and the Lions Clubs do for the mainstream middle class—they provide networks and mentors and personal/business contacts that increase the individual's chance for success and bring influence and prestige to the ethnic group. The list in the *1995 Fra Noi Directory* includes the Arcolian Dental Arts Society, Columbian Club of Chicago, Gregorians (educators), Harlem Avenue Italian and American Business Association, Heart of Italy Association, Italian American Executives of Transportation, Italian American Labor Council, Italian

American Medical Association, Italian American Police Association, and the Italian Midwest Exchange. The Italian American Political Coalition has broader concerns, but it too might be seen as a club for political activists of Italian background. The score of chapters of the Italian American Military Veterans (ITAM) in the Chicago area might also be listed in this category.

A number of Chicago area Italian-American organizations are chapters or affiliates of national groups. They include the Chicago Italian American Chamber of Commerce, Italian American War Veterans, Italian Catholic Federation, Italic Studies Institute, National Italian American Foundation, Order Sons of Italy in America, Pursuing Our Italian Names Together, and UNICO National.

In the 1980s, almost a century after the migration of the grandparents and great-grandparents, Italian Americans around Chicago in large numbers continued to engage in activities that had been pre-determined by their ethnic identity. A sampling of some of the activities over the last decades will serve to illustrate their range and depth: the Mazzini-Verdi Society of mostly Lucchesi businessmen has a Franklin Park clubhouse with carpeted bocce courts; the Maroons Soccer Club draws big crowds at 7 a.m. on Sunday mornings to view soccer matches live from Italy via satellite; at the monthly meetings of the Amaseno Society in Chicago Heights the debate is conducted in four languages (standard Italian, the Amasenese dialect, standard English, and broken English); the JCCIA Young Adults Division plans Wisconsin ski trips and candlelight bowling parties; the Italian American Executives of Transportation organize evenings at the hockey games; the Italo American National Union presents "David Awards" to young professionals based on the promise in their work; the Italian American Chamber of Commerce conducts an annual summer convention/retreat at a Wisconsin resort; the Piedmontese Association plans exchange trips to northern Italy and to California to visit colonies of other Piedmontese; the Italian American Sports Hall of Fame regularly calls on Tommy Lasorda as its banquet emcee; the Order Sons of Italy Illinois Grand Lodge holds its annual dinner in a hotel on the weekend before Columbus Day; each Labor Day weekend sees the descendants of immigrants from Alta Villa Milicia celebrate the Feast of Santa Maria Lauretana at Harlem and Cermak complete with a procession and the "flight of the angels" (children suspended on 30-foot high pulleys above the shrine); Paul Basile and his staff put out a 120-page issue each month; Gino and Maria Nuccio of the Italian Radio Theatre have mounted Italian-language plays each year for the past three decades that draw large crowds of adults and children; Casa Italia sponsors a circus; a dozen Italian-language broadcasts hit the airwaves each week from a variety of high- and low-powered AM and FM stations; and the Italian Cultural Center each year mounts an art and history exhibit at the Daley Civic Center to mark Columbus Day.

And that's only scratching the surface! A person could probably attend a "man of the year" dinner dance sponsored by a different Italian-American organization every Saturday night of the year.

If Italian Americans have been sometimes thwarted in their political ambitions, as individuals they have compensated in other fields. The litany of contemporary and historic ethnic achievers and overachievers gives a clear sense of the dynamic roles played by Italian Americans in Chicago society. The list also provides some role models for emerging leaders who will influence the future of the community.

The saintly Mother Cabrini died in the Chicago hospital she founded. The previously mentioned Capone distinguished himself in his field and has become a role model to all too many of his co-nationals. Enrico Fermi was a Chicago Italian. The legendary Serafina Ferrara helped plan thousands of Italian-American weddings in the back room of her Taylor Street bakery. More recent stellar achievers include Dominick De Matteo, who parlayed a small North Side grocery into the gigantic supermarket chain that bears his first name. Cardinal Bernardin was an Italian American who grew up in North Carolina. Dino D'Angelo, born in Castel di Sangro in the 1920s, conquered depression, then created a real estate empire that included the Civic Opera House. D'Angelo's philanthropy toward various universities and hospitals approaches the $10 million mark.

Our list continues with Federal Judge Nicholas Bua, whose courageous decisions outlawed political coercion of city and county employees. Virginio Ferrari, a Veronese minimalist sculptor, is the creator of one of the most visible art works in the city, "Being Born," which is located at Orleans Street and the Ohio entrance to the Kennedy Expressway. Theresa Petrone is a member of the City Board of Elections. Professor Robert Remini of the University of Illinois at Chicago was the winner of the American Book Award for nonfiction for his three-volume biography of Andrew Jackson. Dominick Buffalino is the former chair of the Board of Governors, which ran some five universities in the state. Leonard Amari served as executive director of the Illinois Bar Association. Fred Gardaphé's list of publications and presentations on Italian-American literature is enormous. Joseph Marchetti, a patron of the arts and Ferrari automobiles, headed the family that ran one of Chicago's most popular restaurants, the venerable Como Inn. Anthony Terlato brought Santa Margherita Pinot Grigio to the American market. Several Italian-named persons read us the evening news and sports on major Chicago television stations, and "Holy Cow!" Harry Caray, the legendary baseball announcer for the Cubs, was an Italian American. The list of Italian American achievers is longer, but the point is clear that there is an abundance of Italian Americans achieving at the very highest levels of Chicago society. And to varying degrees, each of these leaders maintained a degree of *Italianitá* that they transmit to the public and—more importantly—back to the Italian-American community. In their lifestyles and through ethnic media such as *Fra Noi*, these prominent Chicago Italians, along with the more humble community-based organizations, reinforce Italian-American ethnicity in Chicago.

Conclusion

There are in the Chicago area about 300,000 Italian Americans of various generations, which is the population of a medium-sized Italian city. Economically, they have entered the American mainstream and are solidly middle class, with incomes higher than those of most urban ethnic groups. Although probably fewer than five percent of them use Italian as their first language, most Italian Americans know a few phrases in the language, and the registration of third- and fourth-generation young people in high school and college Italian classes is slowly increasing. And despite the exogamy rate (outmarriage to non-Italians) of about 50 percent, a solid sense of Italian-ness still persists. The typical Chicago Italian American is now in the third or fourth generation and has given up the inner city for suburban locations.

Strong family bonding and family orientation are still highly cherished values even in the third generation. Though the group has been represented in the city for over a century, it continues to maintain a lively array of social, cultural, and religious institutions and organizations that provide a sense of ethnic identification and recognition in a manageable arena within the large metropolis. Because the institutions perform the psychic function of allocating recognition, they will not die or fade quickly from the scene. New initiatives on the part of the Italian government will enhance the "high culture" aspect of Italian-American ethnicity. Moreover, the tolerant cultural climate for all ethnicities in the city, and the increased interest among third and fourth generations in ethnic roots and travel to Italy, will maintain Italian-American ethnic presence in Chicago for generations to come.

BIBLIOGRAPHY

Allswang, John. *A House for All Peoples: Ethnic Politics in Chicago, 1890–1936*. Lexington, KY: University of Kentucky Press, 1971.

Bell, Daniel. "Crime as an American Way of Life: A Queer Ladder of Social Mobility" in *The End of Ideology: on the Exhaustion of Political Ideas in the Fifties*. New York: Free Press 1962.

Bernardi, Adria. *Houses with Names*, Urbana, IL: University of Illinois Press, 1990.

Bulletin (1908–present). Italian American Chamber of Commerce of Chicago.

Candeloro, Dominic. "The Role of the Scalabrini Fathers in the Chicago Italian American Community" in *To See the Past More Clearly: The Enrichment of the Italian Heritage, 1890–1990*. New York: American Italian Historical Association: 1994.

———. *Images of America: Italians in Chicago*. Charleston, SC: Arcadia, 1999.

———. "Italians in Chicago: The Ethnic Factor" in *Ethnic Chicago*. Revised ed. Grand Rapids, MI: Eerdmans, 1995.

———. "Suburban Italians: Chicago Heights, 1890–1975" in *Ethnic Chicago*. Revised and expanded ed. Grand Rapids, MI: Eerdmans, 1984.

———. *Voices of America: Italians in Chicago*. Charleston, SC: Arcadia, 2001.

Chicago Tribune, online (1985–present).

Church Anniversary books of Our Lady of Mount Carmel, Our Lady of Pompeii, St. Anthony of Padua. Available at the Italian Cultural Center, Chicago.

Cowan, David and John Kuenster. *To Sleep with the Angels*. Chicago: Ivan R. Dee, 1996.

Cutler, Irving. *Chicago: Metropolis of Mid-Continent*. 3rd ed. Dubuque, IA: Kendall Hunt, 1982.

De Rosa, Tina. *Bishop John Baptist Scalabrini: Father to the Migrants*. Chicago: Insider Publishers, 1987.

———. *Paper Fish*. New York: The Feminist Press, 1980.

De Vita, Salvatore. *Villa Scalabrini 25th Anniversary Souvenir Book*, 1951–1976. Chicago: 1976.

Ets, Marie Hall. *Rosa: The Life of an Italian Immigrant*. Madison: University of Wisconsin Press, 1970.

Fra Noi (1960–present). Italian Cultural Center. Stone Park, IL.

Fermi, Laura. *Atoms in the Family*. Chicago: University of Chicago Press, 1995.

Gardaphé, Fred. *Mustache Pete is Dead.* West LaFayette, IN: Bordighera, 1997.

H-ItAm listserv searchable archive at http://www2.h-net.msu.edu/~itam/.

Ianni, Francis. *Black Mafia: Ethnic Succession in Organized Crime.* New York: Simon and Schuster, 1974.

"Immigrants in the Cities." United States Immigration Commission Reports (Dillingham Report), Volume 26. 1911.

Kobler, John. *Life and World of Al Capone.* New York: Da Capo Press, 1971.

LaGumina, Salvatore, et al. *The Italian American Experience: An Encyclopedia.* New York: Garland, 2000.

La Parola del Popolo (1908–1983). Chicago.

La Tribuna Transatlantica (1898–1924). Chicago.

Lettieri,Vincenzo. *Tales of the Immigrant.* Consenza, Italy: Edizioni Brenner, 2001.

L'Italia (1880s–1930s). Chicago.

Mangione, Jerre and Ben Morreale. *La Storia.* New York: Harper, 1992

Miller, Eugene and Gianna Panofsky. *Struggling in Chicago, Italian Immigrants with a Socialist Agenda.* Unpublished manuscript: 2000.

Nelli, Humbert. *The Business of Crime.* New York: Oxford Press, 1976.

———. *Italians in Chicago, 1880–1930.* New York: Oxford Press, 1970.

Pero, Peter. "A Brief History of the Italians in Chicago's Labor Movement," unpublished essay, 1978.

Photo archives of the *Fra Noi.* Casa Italia, Stone Park, IL.

Photo archives of the *Chicago Daily News* Online. Chicago Historical Society.

Schiavo, Giovanni. *The Italians in Chicago: A Study in Americanization.* New York: Arno Press, 1975.

Sorrentino, Anthony. *Organizing Against Crime: Redeveloping the Neighborhood.* New York: Human Sciences Press, 1977.

———. *Organizing the Ethnic Community: An Account of the Origin, History and Development of the Joint Civic Committee of Italian Americans 1952–1995.* New York: Center for Migration Studies, 1995.

Vecoli, Rudolph. "Prelates and Peasants." *Journal of Social History* 2 (1969): 217–268.

———. *Chicago's Italians Prior to World War I.* (unpublished Ph.D. dissertation). University of Wisconsin: 1963.

Venturelli, Peter. *Acculturation and Persistence of Ethnicity in a Northern Italian District.* (Ph.D. dissertation). University of Chicago: 1981.

———. "Institutions in an Ethnic District." *Human Organization* 41 (1982): 26–35.

Zummo, Bruce. *Little Sicily: Reminiscences and Reflections of Chicago's Near North Side.* Rosemont, IL: Near North Publishing, 2001.

Taped Oral History Interviews by the author available at the Italian Cultural Center, Stone Park, IL:
Congressman Frank Annunzio, 1983
Egidio Clemente, 1979
Fr. Gino Dalpiaz, 1990
Fr. Armando Pierini, 1983
Joseph De Serto, 1983
Anthony Scariano, 2001
Mariano Turano, 1980s

Transcribed Oral History Interviews (110), 1980, Italians in Chicago Project, Italian Cultural Center, Stone Park.

INDEX